FROM THE ARCHAEOLOGICAL COLLECTIONS OF CRACOW AND JENA

DE REBUS QUIBUSDAM, QUAE IN COLLECTIONIBUS ARCHAEOLOGICIS CRACOVIAE ET IENAE ASSERVANTUR

Redactores

Joachim Śliwa et *Ernst Kluwe*

Sumptibus Universitatis Iagellonicae

Uniwersytet Jagielloński

FROM THE ARCHAEOLOGICAL COLLECTIONS OF CRACOW AND JENA

Edited by

Joachim Śliwa and *Ernst Kluwe*

Nakładem Uniwersytetu Jagiellońskiego

COVER DESIGN
Magda Dębicka

REVIEWERS
Stefan Skowronek
Juliusz Ziomecki

TECHNICAL EDITOR
Henryk Stachowski

PAŃSTWOWE WYDAWNICTWO NAUKOWE
ODDZIAŁ W KRAKOWIE, UL. SŁAWKOWSKA 14
1336
VARIA — tom CCXXXIV
NAKŁADEM UNIWERSYTETU JAGIELLOŃSKIEGO

Wydanie I. Nakład 580+80 egz. Ark. wyd. 6,25. Ark. druk. $4^8/_{16}$ + 10 wkl.
Oddano do składania w marcu 1988 r. Podpisano do druku w listopadzie 1988 r.
Druk ukończono w grudniu 1988 r.
Zam. 121/88   1105   Cena zł 200.—
DRUKARNIA UNIWERSYTETU JAGIELLOŃSKIEGO

ISBN 83-01-08867-2

CONTENTS

Within the framework of cooperation between the Jagellonian University in Cracow and the Friedrich Schiller University in Jena a project has been undertaken in the domain of studies over the ancient civilizations, embracing among other things more important problems from the history of both Universities' archaeological collections and studies over the ancient objects coming from them. The first publication from this domain appeared in print in Jena in 1985 (cf. «Zur Geschichte der klassischen Archäologie Jena — Kraków», Wissenschaftliche Beiträge der Friedrich-Schiller-Universität Jena). The volume of studies actually presented is devoted to selected objects from the both centres' archaeological collections. I take a liberty of supposing that also in future, while proceeding with the research over the most interesting archaeological artefacts of Cracow and Jena, a mutual facilitation of respective columns will be possible aimed at publication of the results obtained.

Joachim Śliwa
Jagellonian University

Joachim Śliwa
Kraków

EGYPTIAN AND "EGYPTIANIZING" OBJECTS FROM THE LEO D. KOSTKA COLLECTION IN THE NATIONAL MUSEUM IN CRACOW *

In recent times, shortly after publication of the catalogue of Egyptian scarabs and related objects in the Cracow collections [1], I have unexpectedly encountered in the National Museum in Cracow (Department of the Artistic Handicraft), among the objects of glyptics and goldsmithery, also a certain number of Egyptian scarabs and scaraboids coming, among others, from the former collection of Leo D. Kostka [2].

Leo Kostka (born July 24th, 1871 in Przemyśl, died March 12th, 1948 in Cracow) was a renown for his passion art collector who, towards the end of his life, handed over his entire collection to the National Museum in Cracow [3]. In his antiquarian activity he showed main interest in the field

---

* I wish to acknowledge my debt and gratitude to the managing staff of the National Museum in Cracow in person of Mrs. Jadwiga Bezwińska, Ph. D., as well as to the Curator of Department of Artistic Handicraft Mrs. Stanisława Odrzywolska, M. A., for putting this part of that collection at my disposal and consenting for the publication.

[1] J. Śliwa, *Egyptian Scarabs, Scaraboids and Plaques from the Cracow Collections*. Zeszyty Naukowe UJ 760, Prace Archeologiczne 38, Studia z Archeologii Śródziemnomorskiej 8. Warszawa—Kraków 1985.

[2] The majority of objects of this type comes from the C. Schmidt-Ciążyński collection (incorporated into the National Museum in 1886), much richer and bearing larger scientific importance. Their separate publication is due to appear soon *(Egyptian scarabs and magical gems from the collection of C. Schmidt-Ciążyński)*.

[3] An agreement had been concluded on August, 9th, 1947 between him and the Direction of the National Museum in Cracow on strength of which he handed over his collection, since forming a separate department of the Museum named "The Kostka and

of Polish and foreign artistic handiwork, having gathered curious artefacts of silver and ivory, objects of goldwork, rings, gems and cameos, ceramics, pieces of furniture, orders and medals, freemasons' badges, pocket watches (18th and 19th centuries). His collection contained also some 150 oil paintings and water-colours, some 150 drawings, 26 miniatures and 150 specimens of the Japanese art [4]. It should be also pointed out that when staying in Paris towards close of the 19th century, Leo Kostka had attended the *École du Louvre* and, prompted by desire of getting acquainted with works of art, had undertaken travels to Belgium, Switzerland and Italy [5].

Since the L. Kostka collection comprises not many *Aegyptiaca* (Cat. Nos. 1—6) [6], I deem it proper and justified to add here up a couple of objects only indirectly connected with Egypt for sake of their not having fallen into oblivion and division. Of course, they also come from the L. Kostka collection. Two Etruscan scarabs are here in question (cf. Cat. Nos. 7, 8) as well as two gems, from which one proves to be a highly interesting object (Cat. No. 9), and falls into the category of magical amulets, called previously the gnostic gems. The other, however (Cat. No. 10) is a loose imitation coming probably from 17th/18th century and employing hieroglyphic signs as a decorative motif.

We have no more detailed information at hand, concerning the origin of objects from the L. Kostka collection discussed here — they enriched his collection of some 200 gems and cameos [7] as antiquarian acquisitions or objects acquired by means of exchange — and the founder of collection had not left any particulars on more definite circumstances.

Kochanowski Family Collection". At the same time, the Museum committed itself to earmark annually due funds, thus enabling L. Kostka to enlarge and maintain his collection. At the moment of the collection's takeover, the Museum appointed L. Kostka its lifelong keeper.

[4] Cf. materials kept in the Archives of the National Museum in Cracow and the biogram of L. Kostka elaborated by K. Buczkowski (*Polski Słownik Biograficzny* 14, Wrocław—Kraków 1968—1969, p. 351—352).

[5] In Paris, L. Kostka had taken up studies at the College of Commerce and, having returned to Poland, he completed the School of Mining at Borysław. In 1900—1931 he had been employed in the Regional Direction of the State Railways in Cracow, having acted as head of the department for many years. According to K. Buczkowski, the author of the biogram quoted (cf. note 4), "the collecting passion of L. Kostka was based upon modest material means. He supplemented his collection by continuous exchanges and transactions, having himself led an almost indigent life".

[6] Two apparent fakes have been excluded from the collection: 1. spindle — shaped scarab with naturalistically modelled underside, made of chalcedony, with the dimensions of 24.5/15.2/10 mm, Inv. No. MNK IV-Zł-2968 (formerly MNK 160.477.S); 2. flat scarab with non-Egyptian and non-ancient signs on the flat base, made of lapis-lazuli, without the aperture, with the dimensions of 21/16/6.5 mm, Inv. No. MNK IV-Zł-2969 (formerly MNK 160.478.S).

[7] In a list from November, 14th, 1949 there was an entry, among other objects in L. Kostka collection, "Cameos and stones — 212 items" (cf. Archives of the National Museum in Cracow, Dz. p. 165/49).

CATALOGUE

Abbreviations

Jaeger, *Essai* — B. Jaeger, *Essai de classification et datation des scarabées Menkhéperrê.*
  Orbis Biblicus et Orientalis, Series Archaeologica 2. Fribourg-Göttingen
  1982.
LIMC II — *Lexicon Iconographicum Mythologiae Classicae.* Vol. II. München 1984.
Matouk, *Corpus II* — F. S. Matouk, *Corpus du scarabée égyptien. II. Analyse théma-
  tique.* Beyrouth 1977.
Petrie, *BDS* — W. M. F. Petrie, *Button and Design Scarabs.* London 1925.
Skarabäen Basel — E. Hornung, E. Staehelin (ed.), *Skarabäen und andere Siegel-
  amulette aus Basler Sammlungen.* Ägyptische Denkmäler in der Schweiz.
  Band 1. Mainz 1976.
Zazoff, *ES* — P. Zazoff, *Etruskische Skarabäen.* Mainz 1968.

1. Scarab   Pl. I, 1

Inv. No. MNK IV-Zł-2971 (formerly MNK 160.480.S).
Green chlorite slate.
14.6/11/6.6 mm.
State of preservation: very good.
New Kingdom (?).
Bibliography: unpublished.

Fairly high scarab with schematically shaped legs (one incision parallel
to the base's edge, another one slanting) and schematically treated back;
two parallel lines part the *prothorax*, one engraved line on the axis separates
elytra. Head as a semicircular protuberance. Abdomen slightly uplifted.
Parallel lines separating the *prothorax* are carved in too far and overlap
the surface of legs. Aperture driven alongside the axis.

On the base's surface in an oval enclosure, representation of the
kneeling male figure is engraved, clad in the short loin-cloth. Head rendered
schematically with the profile simplified and long hair falling on the
shoulders to the rear. Hands stretched forward up to the height of the face.
In the space between the knees and elbows the *t* sign is engraved. Engraving
lines are fairly deep, schematic. No parallel. Features of shaping of the
scarab's back and legs enable its numbering among the New Kingdom
objects.

2. Scarab
Pl. I, 2

Inv. No. MNK IV-Zł-2973 (formerly MNK 160.482.S).
Pale beige slate.
9/7/4 mm.
State of preservation: very good.
New Kingdom.
Bibliography: unpublished.

Miniature, very carefully made scarab on a low base. Legs treated in naturalistic way with their upper surface covered by tiny, regular incisions. Back carefully shaped with a distinct contraction clearly marked at the joint of *prothorax* and *elytra*. The *prothorax* is oval, circumlined from inside by a single engraved line. Similar line encircles from inside the edges of *elytra*, while double engraved line separates the wing cases. Head in a form of small protuberance clinging to the *prothorax*; *clypeus* large and broad, terminating in four protrusions. Aperture driven alongside the object's axis.

On the base's surface in an oval enclosure, four hieroglyphic signs are carefully carved: *nb* closing the decorative field from below, centrally situated *nfr* sign and symmetrically placed ʿnḫ signs at its both sides. No exact parallel.

Cf.: The signs appearing on the base can be regarded as a graphic variant of a wishing formula "Alles Gute und (alles) Leben", according to the reading proposed by the Basel team: *Skarabäen Basel*, No. Va 15, also there specification of scarabs and scaraboids with analogous arrangement of signs.

3. Scarab
Pl. I, 3

Inv. No. MNK IV-Zł-2972 (formerly MNK 160.481.S).
Slate, green glaze.
12.6/9/6.3 mm.
State of preservation: good.
New Kingdom.
Bibliography: unpublished.

High, rather neglectfully shaped scarab, with legs schematically rendered by means of a single horizontal incision aside, widened halfway its length. Back is circumlined with a single engraved line, while a curved engraved line separates *prothorax* and *elytra*; triangular incisions appear close to the corners of wing cases. Coarse, neglectfully led line separates the wing cases. Head and *clypeus* rendered not very carefully, traces of two incisions are visible on the edge of *clypeus*. Aperture driven alongside the axis.

On the base's surface in an oval enclosure, not very careful representations are engraved of two pacing falcon-headed deities, facing right. Hands let loosely down the body. Above these two figures, a solar disc is engraved with uraei on both sides. Undoubtedly, a pair of solar deities is concerned here. An identical arrangement of figures is lacking (only Matouk, *Corpus II*, 254, p. 337, but the deity on the left has a separated solar disc, while a crescent appears above the head of the deity on the right). Most often, such figures with falcon heads, surmounted by solar discs, happen to compose an element of the triad with Amun in the centre — in this case heads of both flanking deities face one another (cf. *Skarabäen Basel*, Nos. 655, 656 and parallels confronted there).

4. Scarab
Pl. I, 4

Inv. No. MNK IV-Zł-2967 (formerly MNK 160.476.S).
Amethist.
17.7/12/9.2 mm.
State of preservation: considerably abraded surface and edges of the object.
New Kingdom.
Bibliography: unpublished.

High, neglectfully made scarab. Body separated from the high base by two parallel incisions running around. On the surface of the back delimitation between *prothorax* and *elytra* marked by an engraved line and — parallel to the object's axis — a parting line of the wing cases. *Prothorax* merging with the head shaped in a very summary way. Aperture driven alongside the object's axis.

On the base's surface in an oval enclosure engraved signs *mn-ḫpr-rˁ* (the *nsw-bjt* name of Tuthmosis III or cryptographic record of the Amun's name). According to the classification of Jaeger, *Essai*, § 37, ordinary writing form of type 1. a 1°. No parallels (on the problems connected with the scarabs of type *Mn-ḫpr-rˁ* see Jaeger, *Essai*). The way of the entire object's workmanship, material as well as details of hieroglyphic signs' elaboration (particularly the *ḫpr* sign!) indicate the non-Egyptian origin of the scarab (Syria, Palestine?)

5. Cowroid

 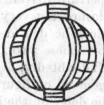

Inv. No. MNK IV-Zł-2974 (formerly MNK 160.483.S).
Slate, green glaze.
Diameter 12, height 5 mm.
State of preservation: good.
Early New Kingdom (XVIIIth Dynasty).
Bibliography: unpublished.

Cowroid of an untypical shape — on a low round base the cowroid proper with the edges decorated by parallel incisions (inner lines filled with the ladder pattern), with a free "lens" left on the axis. Aperture driven at the object's axis, its ends placed in special cylindrical protrusions.

On the surface of distinctly roundly delineated base, in a circular rim engraved by means of compasses, there is a four-petal rosette emerging from a small circle in the centre — in the spaces between regularly distributed petals there are carefully engraved lines terminating in spiral and tiny leaf, the latter running in an opposite direction.

Cf.: Petrie, *BDS*, Pl. X, 431; W. M. F. Petrie, E. Mackay, G. Wainwright. *Meydum and Memphis III*. London 1910, Pl. XXVII, 85; Matouk, *Corpus II*, p. 408, No. 2215; *Skarabäen Basel*, No. 674 (cowroid of identical shape: "helm"artige und von zwei schraffierten Bändern umrahmte Form).

6. Bug

Inv. No. MNK IV-Zł-2970 (formerly MNK 160.479.S).
Brown slate.
22.8/18/8.8 mm.
State of preservation: very good.
Late Period.
Bibliography: unpublished.

Object without a typical base, yet with a naturalistically shaped lower part. Back shaped schematically, distinctly engraved horizontal lines separate the head from *prothorax* and the *prothorax* from *elytra*; single line parts the wing cases. The bug's edge, both in the section of *clypeus* and that of abdomen, covered by regular incisions each on left and right side at the level of partition between *prothorax* and *elytra*. At the bottom, the modelling designed to render the bug's underside made very schematically and neglectfully by means of slanting incisions. Aperture for hanging up driven in a centrally situated protuberance at the bottom, transversely to the object's axis.

Cf.: *Skarabäen Basel*, No. 915.

*

* *

PLATE I

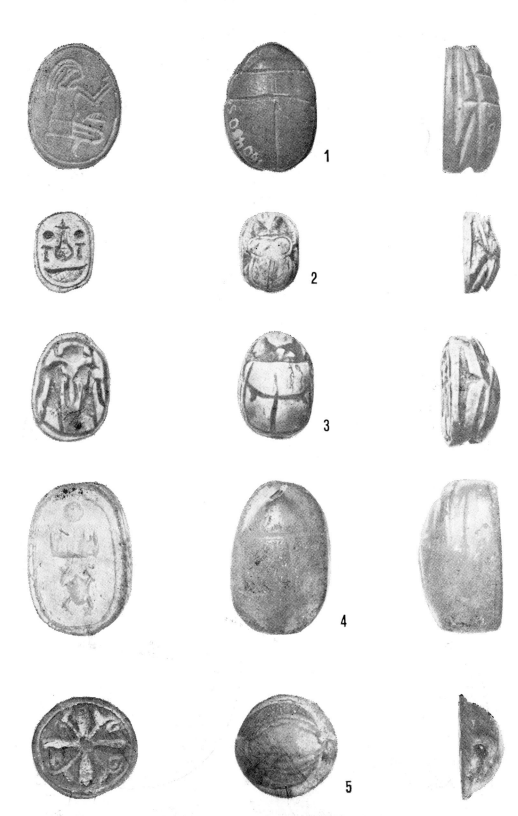

PLATE II

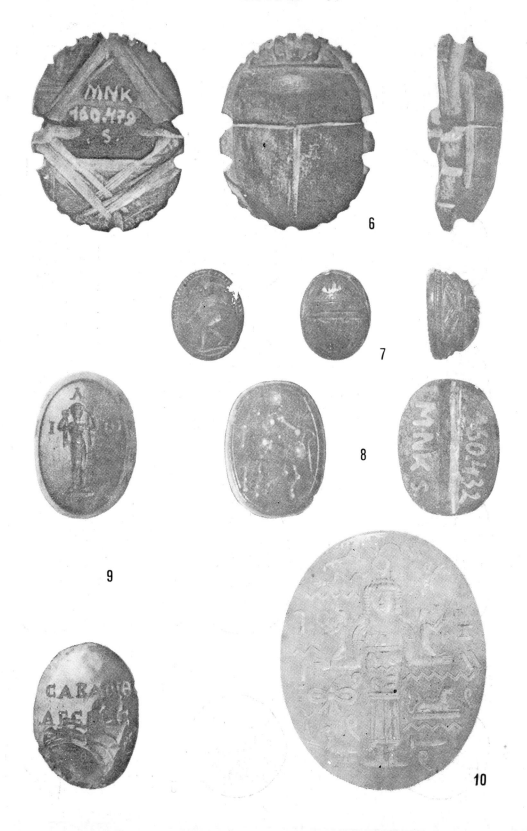

6

7

8

9

10

7. Base of a scarab

Inv. No. MNK IV-Zł-2919 (formerly MNK 160.432.S).
Cornelian.
15/11/3.5 mm.
State of preservation: only the scarab's base is preserved, purposely cut off.
Late Etruscan (*a globolo* style); late 4th/early 3rd century B. C.
Bibliography: unpublished.

On the upper surface of the intentionally cut off base the remainder
of the aperture is visible driven once alongside the scarab's axis. Fairly
deeply carved line runs around the base, also three slanting incisions each
discernible on both left and right side of the base, intended to mark the
bug's legs.

On the base's surface, in an oval engraved rim, a figure is represented
of a centaur facing left, with a torso slightly inclined back, holding
a schematically rendered bough. The representation of the centaur is
made in a typical "a globolo" style (cf. Zazoff, *ES*, p. 118 ff. and
E. Zwierlein-Diehl, *Antike Gemmen in Deutschen Sammlungen*. Bd. II:
Berlin, München 1969, p. 112: *Rundperl-Stil*) and has an excellent counter-
part in Etruscan scarab from the Stosch collection in Berlin (its legs have
been marked in the same way as in the case of the Cracow object).

Cf.: Cornelian scarab in the Stosch collection, Berlin (Zazoff, *ES*, No. 901 and
E. Zwierlein-Diehl, *Antike Gemmen in Deutschen Sammlungen*. Bd. II: *Berlin*,
München 1969, No. 257 and the literature quoted there).

8. Scarab

Inv. No. MNK IV-Zł-2966 (formerly MNK 160.475.S).
Cornelian.
10/8.1/5.8 mm.
State of preservation: very good.
Late Etruscan or Italic, 4th—3rd century B. C.
Bibliography: unpublished.

On a low base surrounded by the "Strichband", a fairly high scarab is
modelled by means of incisions and engraved lines. Legs marked as slanting,
double parallel incisions. *Prothorax* separated by means of two parallel
lines, its outer edge additionally decorated by a series of tiny incisions.
Clypeus marked very schematically. The wing cases separated by two
parallel lines. In the corners of the wing cases, instead of usual "triangles",
a series of parallel vertical incisions. Aperture driven alongside the object's
axis.

On the base's surface in a narrow frame taken up by regularly
distributed strokes ("Strichrand"), a male figure is represented facing left
and standing on the right foot, while the left leg is slightly uplifted. Ground
line. The whole torso is somewhat forward-inclined, which corresponds

14

with the hands' position. The hands hold the ends of a rope running archwise upwards beyond the figure's head.

No exact parallel, yet considering the features of the bug's shaping (cf. Zazoff, *ES*, No. 203) it may be classified with the Late Etruscan objects (Late Etruscan or Italic).

9. Magical amulet

Pl. II, 9

Inv. No. MNK IV-Zł-3033 (formerly MNK 160.131.S).
Cornelian.
19/13.7/5.2 mm.
State of preservation: large chips of stone lacking in the lower part of side B.
2nd—3rd centuries A. D.
Bibliography: unpublished.

SIDE A: engraved representation of Aphrodite Anadyomene situated in the centre of decorative field. Ground line. In the upper part: I A Ω (letters carefully distributed at the apices of a triangle formed by Aphrodite's elbows and head top).

SIDE B: two lines of text,

CABAWΘ
ΑΓΕΤ[...]C

of which the second is uncertain because it wholly lacks the penultimate letter, its second letter was probably Γ, its fourth was presumably Τ (ΑΓΕΤΟC "splendid, marvellous, admirable"). Possibly a third line of the text may have appeared below and been lost by splintering.

EDGE: on the narrow oblique surface of the gem, at the left side the letters PBI, and on the right side the letters ΛΡΗΛ are engraved (probably to be read alternately as PΛBPIHΛ [coming from ΓABPIHΛϡ]).

Among the magical gems, this piece is an example of the so-called love talismans. Aphrodite Anadyomene may have been associated with the goddess Hathor in Egypt; on another gem, before a commonplace epithet of Aphrodite αρωριφρασις, we find the name of Hathor: AΘWP (cf. E. Drioton, *Notes diverses, 12. Aphrodite Anadyomène invoquée comme Hathor.* ASAE XLV, 1947, p. 82—83).

Cf.: A. Delatte, Ph. Derchain, *Les intailles magiques gréco-égyptiennes.* Paris 1964, p. 183—189; M.-O. Jentel, *LIMC II,* 1984, p. 156—157, Nos. 40—66; A. Krug, *Antike Gemmen im Römisch-Germanischen Museum Köln.* Bericht der Römisch-Germanischen Kommission 61, 1980, No. 287. Concerning Iao and Sabaoth: *Der Kleine Pauly 2,* 1979, Col. 1314—1319 and C. Bonner, *Studies in Magical Amulets, chiefly Graeco-Egyptian.* Ann Arbor 1950, p. 30, 134—135, 170, 196 and lastly H. Philipp, *Mira et Magica,* Mainz 1986, p. 22. On the Gabriel — Bonner, *Studies...,* p. 170, 214; Philipp, *Mira et Magica,* p. 94 (see also for magical gems in general, with latest bibliography).

10. Gem

Inv. No. MNK IV-Zł-2954 (formerly MNK 160.467.S).
Cornelian.
29/23.3/5.2 mm.
State of preservation: very good.
France or Italy, 17th—18th century (?).
Bibliography: unpublished.

An oval gem, one side decorated by a sunken engraved line. Central part of the field occupied by a frontally disposed female figure in a long garment. Arms at elbows bent outward horizontally. Wig on the head with its tips falling down upon shoulders. Above the figure and on both sides, an inapt imitation of some Egyptian hieroglyphs (most of them have counterparts among the Egyptian signs, but one is a simplified picture of a butterfly!).

Both the figure's features and its arrangement, as well as the way of rendering the hieroglyphic signs, fail to display the skill and sense of the basic elements found in that Egyptian style, which the artist strove to follow. Object without parallel, it may have originated in France or Italy in 17th/18th centuries or later.

Joachim Oelsner
Jena

INSCHRIFTEN MITTELELAMISCHER, NEUASSYRISCHER UND NEUBABYLONISCHER HERRSCHER AUF ZIEGELN IN KRAKÓW UND JENA

Die National-Museen in Kraków und die Hilprecht-Sammlung Vorderasiatischer Altertümer der Friedrich-Schiller-Universität Jena besitzen einige beschriftete Ziegel, die im Interesse einer möglichst vollständigen Erfassung des Materials aus dem alten Vorderasien mitgeteilt werden sollen, obwohl sie kaum etwas Neues enthalten. Die Objekte in Kraków konnten während zweier Aufenthalte 1981 und 1985 studiert werden. Für die Genehmigung zur Veröffentlichung sei den Museumsdirektionen gedankt, für die Unterstützung der Arbeit den Mitarbeiterinnen des Czartoryski-Museums und des Archäologischen Museums. Besonderer Dank gilt Kollegen Dozent Dr. Joachim Śliwa, der mich auf die Texte aufmerksam machte und ihr Studium im Museum vorbereitete.

I

Die kleine Sammlung altorientalischer Stücke der *Zbiory Czartoryskich* enthält neben einigen Rollsiegeln [1], einem neubabylonischen Tonzylinder mit Inschrift Nebukadnezars II (604—562) [2], wenigen Tontafeln [3] auch

---

[1] Veröffentlicht von S. Przeworski, Archiv für Orientforschung 3 (1926), 172—174; 5 (1928/29), 23 mit Anm. 1 und Taf. IX, 3; 9 (1933/34), 122 f.

[2] Vgl. J. Zabłocka, *Napis Nabuchodonozora II o budowie Starego Pałacu*, Zeszyty Naukowe Uniwersytetu im. Adama Mickiewicza, Historia — Zeszyt 7 (1967), 102—117; dies. und P.-R. Berger, *Ein vollständiges Duplikat zur Nebukadnezar-Inschrift VAB 4 Nr. 46*, Orientalia NS 38 (1969), 122—125.

[3] Publiziert wurden zwei altassyrische Texte von L. Matouš, *Deux tablettes cappodociennes de la collection des Czartoryski à Cracovie*, Archeologia 8 (Warschau 1956),

einige Fragmente neuassyrischer Provenienz. Von diesen wurde das wichtigste Stück, ein Reliefbruchstück, bereits vor längerer Zeit veröffentlicht [4]. Einige weitere, ziemlich unbedeutende Stein-Fragmente sind noch unpubliziert. Es handelt sich um drei kleine, beschriftete Beispiele, von denen das grösste (Inv.-Nr. MNK XI 622a) neben der Keilschrift auch Reste einer bildlichen Darstellung aufweist, die beiden anderen (MNK XI 622b) zeigen nur einige Schriftzeichen. Die Bestimmung ist noch nicht gelungen, ebensowenig kann ein Fragment einer glasierten Knauffliesse (MNK XI 619) mit Inschriftresten zugeordnet werden [5].

Die beiden Reliefstücke Nr. 622b sind zusammen mit drei Ziegelfragmenten in einem Kasten eingegipst. Von den letzteren enthalten zwei nur noch vereinzelte Zeichen (Reste von 5 bzw. 2 Zeilen, nicht identifiziert), ein grösseres Stück (Höhe 8, Breite 11,5 cm) gehört zu einem Ziegel Salmanassars III (858—824). Der Fundort ist nicht bekannt. Der Text ist aus Assur und Ninive bezeugt und hier in folgender Weise angeordnet:

É. ⌈GAL⌉ ᵐᵈŠ[ùl-ma-nu-MAŠ MAN ŠÚ MAN ᴷᵁᴿAš(-šur)]
A Aš-šur-PAB-A [MAN ŠÚ MAN ᴷᵁᴿAš(-šur)]
A TUKUL-MAŠ MAN ᴷᵁ[ᴿAš-šur-ma]

„Palast des S[almanassar, des Königs der Gesamtheit, Königs des Landes Assur], des Sohnes des Assurnasirpal, [des Königs der Gesamtheit, Königs des Landes Assur], des Sohnes des Tukulti-Ninurta, Königs des La[ndes Assur]" [6].

---

415 ff.; ders., *Zwei „kappadokische" Tontafeln im Nationalmuseum zu Kraków*, Journal of Juristic Papyrology 11/12 (1958/59), 111—118. Unveröffentlicht ist eine Ur III-Tafel (Inventar-Nr. MNK XI-A-846; Amar-Sin Jahr 2, aus Umma). Erwähnung verdienen ferner drei Tonnägel Gudeas von Lagasch (ca. 2143—2124 v. u. Z.): MNK XI-1206 und 1207 (Text identisch mit Backstein A = F. Thureau-Dangin, *Die sumerischen und akkadischen Königsinschriften*, Leipzig 1907 (Vorderasiatische Bibliothek 1), 140 f.) sowie MNK XI-1208 (Text identisch mit Backstein F = ebd. 142 f.).

[4] S. Przeworski, *Ein assyrisches Relieffragment aus einer krakauer Sammlung*, Rocznik Orientalistyczny 6 (1928), 84—88.

[5] Zum Typ vgl. W. Andrae, *Farbige Keramik aus Assur*, Berlin 1923, 28—34, Taf. 31—34, s. auch AfO 9 (1933/34), 79. — Erhalten ist von der Inschrift: ...] x MAN ᴷᵁᴿAŠ(= Aššur)-ma NÍG.GA É ᵈNIN-[... "...]. des Königs des Landes Assur. Besitz des Tempels der Gottheit Nin[... (Ninurta, Ninlil?)".

[6] Nachweis der bekannten Exemplare bei W. Schramm, *Einleitung in die assyrischen Königsinschriften II*, Leiden/Köln 1973 (Handbuch der Orientalistik, 1. Abt., Erg. bd. 5), 95 Nr. 26, 96 Nr. 6, vgl. S. 98 sub j am Ende; Übersetzung: D. D. Luckenbill, *Ancient Records of Assyria and Babylonia I*, Chicago 1926, 249 § 693 f.; dem Keilschrifttext (gestempelt) entspricht am besten das Exemplar bei O. Schroeder, *Keilschrifttexte aus Assur historischen Inhalts II*, Leipzig 1922, Nr. 105, weiteres Beispiel L. Jakob-Rost/J. Marzahn, *Vorderasiatische Schriftdenkmäler*(= VS) 23 (NF 7), Berlin 1985, Nr. 110, vgl. auch dieselben, *Die Inschriften der assyrischen Könige auf Ziegeln aus Assur I*, Berlin 1985, 319—323.

II

In dem Aufsatz *Historische Texte der Hilprecht-Sammlung*[7] wurden unter Nr. 33 und 35 auch Ziegelinschriften des 1. Jahrt. v. u. Z. aufgeführt. Während zum ersten Text (Ziegel mit Inschrift des Königs Assur-etel-ilani, nach 626)[8] nur noch Farbe (gelblich) und Tiefe (6 cm; Breite des Schriftspiegels 8 cm) nachzutragen wären, sei die Beschreibung der Nebu-kadnezar-Ziegel ergänzt, da sie im Katalog der neubabylonischen Königs-inschriften von P.-R. Berger keine Aufnahme gefunden haben.

Zunächst sei jedoch HS 2981 erwähnt, Ziegelbruchstück mit Inschrift Assurbanipals (668-nach 631) in sumerischer Sprache, Duplikat zu BE[9] 1/I Nr. 82 (17,5 × 9,0 × 2,5 cm, Schriftspiegel 6,5 × 14,5 cm, rötlichbraun, rechte untere Ecke abgebrochen, dadurch Enden von Z. 9—11 verloren)[10]. Das Exemplar (aus Nippur) befand sich im Besitz von Dr. Inez Bernhardt und kam nach ihrem Tode im Jahre 1982 in die Hilprecht-Sammlung.

Die Vorlage für den Gipsabguß HS 2012 (32 × 32 × 7 cm, Schrift-spiegel 9,5 × 15 cm) konnte bis jetzt nicht identifiziert werden. Wie bei

[7] Verf. in: Wissenschaftliche Zeitschrift der Friedrich-Schiller-Universität Jena, Gesellschafts- und Sprachwiss. Reihe, 18 H. 5 (1969) 51—55. Seitdem wurden einige weitere Texte als zugehörig identifiziert: Zu Nr. 8 (= HS 1954+1955) konnten HS 2499 und 2506 zugefügt werden; die Tafel mit 6 Kolumnen auf der Vorderseite und 5 auf der Rückseite ist damit in ihrer ursprünglichen Größe wiedergewonnen, die Oberfläche jedoch teilweise abgebrochen bzw. schwer lesbar, da abgeschabt. HS 1712 enthält Abschriften sumerischer Königsinschriften der Ur III-Zeit (ca. 2112—2004), zu lesen ist der Name Ur-Nammu. HS 1366: Abschrift einer Siegellegende (auf Tontafel) mit Weihung an Schulgi (ARAD-zu-Typ). Zu vgl. ist auch HS 1364: Teil einer privaten Weihinschrift (?) mit Weihung für „das Leben Schu-Sins (Anfang und Ende verloren). Ergänzungen zu einigen weiteren Texten im o. genannten Artikel — Nr. 7: Inv.-Nr. jetzt HS 193; Nr. 10: Inv.-Nr. jetzt 194b, publiziert von A. Westenholz und J. Oelsner, *Zu den Weihplattenfragmenten der Hilprecht-Sammlung Jena*, Altorientalische Forschungen 10, 1983, 212—216; Nr. 12: die wenigen Reste der rechten Kolumne, die erhalten sind, erweisen sich als zur akkadischen Version der sumerischen Inschrift auf der linken Kolumne gehörig, jüngere Abschrift im archaisierenden Duktus; Nr. 24 (HS 1960): veröffentlicht in: Altorientalische Forschungen a. a. O.; Nr. 26: nach Zufügung eines Fragments läßt sich HS 2007 als Sprichwortsammlung bestimmen.

[8] Veröffentlicht von D. O. Edzard, Archiv für Orientforschung 19 (1959/60), 143 (mit Photo), s. Wiss. Zeitschr. Jena (o. Anm. 7) Nr. 33, HS 2985).

[9] = *The Babylonian Expedition of the University of Pennsylvania*, Series A: *Cuneiform Texts*, Philadelphia 1893 ff.

[10] Übersetzt von D. D. Luckenbill (o. Anm. 6) II, 405 Nr. 4 (§ 1121). Zum formalen Aufbau vgl. Edzard in dem o. Anm. 8 genannten Beitrag. Weitere Duplikate wurden unlängst veröffentlicht von C. B. F. Walker, *Cuneiform Brick Inscriptions in the British Museum; the Ashmolean Museum, Oxford; the City of Birmingham Museums and Art Gallery; the City of Bristol Museum and Art Gallery*, London 1981, Nr. 80. Eine weitere, bisher unkannte sumerische Inschrift hat jetzt vorgelegt P. Gerardi, *A New Assurba-nipal Brick Inscription from Nippur*, Annual Review of the Royal Inscriptions of Meso-potamia Project 4 (Toronto 1986) 37.

2*

allen 6-zeiligen Ziegelinschriften Nebukadnezars besteht der Text aus der vollen Titulatur mit Personalpronomen (= A_p (b'') bei Berger) [11]:

$^dN\grave{A}$-ku-dúr-ri-ŠEŠ
LUGAL Ba-bi-lu^{KI}
3 za-ni-in É-sag-il
ù É-zi-da DUMU.UŠ
SAG.KAL šá $^dN\grave{A}$-DUMU.UŠ-ŠEŠ
6 LUGAL Ba-bi-lu^{ki} ana-ku

„(1) Nebukadnezar, (2) König von Babylon, (3) Erhalter von Esagil (4) und Ezida, (5) erstgeborener (4) Sohn (5) des Nabupolassar, (6) des Königs von Babylon, (bin) ich".

HS 2013 ($15{,}7 \times 19 \times 8$ cm, Schriftspiegel $11 \times 14{,}5$ cm, graubraun) trägt eine 7-zeilige Inschrift ohne Personalpronomen (= A (b'') nach Berger). Der Text weist folgende Varianten gegenüber HS 2012 (s. o.) auf: Z. 1: -du-úr- statt dúr, Z. 2 und 7: KÁ.DINGIR.RA^{KI}, Z. 3: -nin statt -ni-in und -il(a) statt -il, Z. 5: a-ša-ri-du.

Der Fundort von HS 2013 ist nicht bekannt. Es ist nicht auszuschließen, das es sich um den Ziegel handelt, den der Botaniker Carl Haussknecht in den 60-er Jahren des 19. Jhs. in Borsippa gefunden hat. In einem heute in der Hilprecht-Sammlung befindlichen Verzeichnis von Gegenständen, die dieser Forschungsreisende [12] aus dem Orient mitgebracht hat, wird an erster Stelle genannt „Backstein mit Keilschrift von Birs Nimrud (Thurm v. Babel)". Ein gleichlautender Zettel befindet sich jedoch bei einem anderen, heute als HS 2918 inventarisierten Stück. Es ist dies die rechte Hälfte eines Ziegels mit elamischer Inschrift des Schutruk-Nahhunte I. (12. Jh. v. u. Z.), die auf Umwegen in die Hilprecht-Sammlung gelangte. Da dieses Exemplar keinesfalls aus Borsippa stammen kann, wird es sich dabei wohl um Nr. 2 des genannten Verzeichnisses handeln: „Backstein von Susa mit Keilschrift" [13]. Die beigelegten Zettel scheinen also irgendwann verwechselt worden zu sein. Da nicht zu beweisen ist, daß HS 2013 zu Hilprechts Nachlaß gehörte, könnte es sich um jenes Exemplar

---

[11] S. P.-R. Berger, *Die neubabylonischen Königsinschriften* [I], Kevelaer/Neukirchen-Vluyn 1973 (Alter Orient und Altes Testament 4/1), 22 (Klassifizierung der Inschriften, vgl. insgesamt S. 19—24), Übersicht über die bekannten Exemplare (gilt auch für das Folgende) ebd. 179 ff.

[12] Carl Haussknecht (1838—1903) unternahm zwei Forschungsreisen zwischen 1863 und 1869, die ihn über Südosteuropa nach Vorderasien (Anatolien, Syrien, Mesopotamien) und Iran führten (freundliche Mitteilung von Dr. Karl Meyer, Leiter des Herbarium Haussknecht, Friedrich-Schiller-Universität Jena). Dabei besuchte er auch alte Ruinenstätten.

[13] In die Hilprecht-Sammlung kam außerdem Nr. 23 des Verzeichnisses: „Säulenstück aus den Ruinen von Hierapolis, Mesopotamien", heute HS 2919 (Höhe 14,5 cm, ursprünglicher Durchmesser etwa 12 cm, aus grauem Stein, verziert mit halbrunden Wülsten).

handeln, das Hausknecht mitgebracht hat. Im anderen Falle muß dieses als verloren betrachtet werden [14].

Der soeben erwähnte elamische Ziegel HS 2918 enthält die Enden der 5-zeiligen Inschrift des genannten Herrschers. Der geschriebene, nicht gestempelte Text weist keine Varianten auf [15].

III

Fünf Nebukadnezar-Ziegel besitzt auch das Archäologische Museum in Kraków. Es sind dies:

1. MAK/AS/118 (33 × 33,5 × 7,5 cm, Schriftspiegel 10,6 × 14,2 cm, graubraun): 7-zeilige Inschrift ohne Personalpronomen [Titulatur A (b'')], Schreibung identisch mit HS 2013.

2. MAK/AS/119 (32,5 × 32,5 × 7 cm, Schriftspiegel 10,8 × 13,8 cm, graubraun): 7-zeilige Inschrift wie das soeben genannte Stück, identisch mit HS 2013.

3. MAK/AS/120 (32 × 32 × 9,5 cm, Schriftspiegel 9,5 × 15,5 cm, gelbrötlich): 6-zeilige Inschrift, identisch mit HS 2012.

4. MAK/AS/172 (32,5 × 33 × 8,5 cm, Schriftspiegel 8,5 × 14,5 cm, graubraun): 6-zeilige Inschrift (Titulatur A_p(b'')) mit Varianten: Z. 2 und 6: *Ba-bi-i-lu^{KI}*, Z. 5 nur *DUMU* statt *DUMU.UŠ ašarīdu(SAG.KAL) ša.*

5. MAK/AS/173 (33 × 33,5 × 8 cm, Schriftspiegel 5,5 × 22,5 cm, graubraun): 3-zeilige Inschrift (Titulatur A(b'')) mit einer von den vorherigen Beispielen mehrfach abweichenden Schreibweise:

$^dN\dot{A}$-*NÍG.DU-ŠEŠ LUGAL KÁ.DIŠ.DI*^{ŠKI} *za-n*[*i*]*n*
É-sag-íla u É-zi-da DUMU.UŠ SAG.KAL
ša $^dN\dot{A}$-*A-ŠEŠ LUGAL KÁ.DINGIR.RA*^{KI} [16].

---

[14] In der Hilprecht-Sammlung befindet sich ferner ein Abklatsch der altpersischen und der elamischen Version der Inschrift des Xerxes (485—465 v. u. Z.) am Berge Elwend, den Haussknecht aufertigte. Nach F. H. Weißbach, *Die Keilinschriften der Achämeniden*, Leipzig 1911 (Vorderasiatische Bibliothek 3), S. XXV sub c, besitzt das Britische Museum einen von [Paul] Haupt 1882 kopierten Papierabdruck der babylonischen Version dieser Inschrift. Gehören die beiden zusammen?

[15] Zugrundegelegt ist die Bearbeitung von F. W. König, *Die elamischen Königsinschriften*, Graz 1965 (Archiv für Orientforschung, Beiheft 16), 71 f. Nr. 18, vgl. S. 13; zum Keilschrifttext s. F. H. Weißbach, *Anzanische Inschriften und Vorarbeiten zu ihrer Entzifferung*, Leipzig 1894 (Abhandl. der philol.-hist. Kl. der Sächs. Akademie der Wiss. 12/2), Taf. I B.

[16] Der Text ist identisch mit VS I 48, bearbeitet von S. Langdon, *Die neubabylonischen Königsinschriften*, Leipzig 1912 (Vorderasiatische Bibliothek 4), 202 f. Nr. 40, vgl. S. 43 (s. auch ebd. Nr. 39 = 4-zeiliger Ziegel und Nr. 41 = 7-zeilig). Zur Schreibung des Namens Babylon als *KÁ.DIŠ.DIŠ = Bāb-ilān s.* R. Borger, *Die Inschriften Asarhaddons, Königs von Assyrien*, Graz 1956 (Archiv für Orientforschung, Beiheft 9), 31.

Der Fundort dieser Exemplare ist nicht bekannt, sie könnten aus Babylon stammen.

Sämtliche in diesem Beitrag vorgestellten Beispiele von Nebukadnezar-Ziegeln sind im archaisierenden Schriftduktus ausgeführt und gestempelt. Sie weisen durchweg Zeilenlinierung auf.

Ewdoksia Papuci-Władyka
Kraków

TWO CORINTHIAN TERRACOTA FIGURINES IN CRACOW

Among the numerous gifts donated by Władysław Czartoryski to the then Archaeological Cabinet of Jagellonian University in 1872, there were, apart from numerous Greek vases, also interesting terracotta figurines [1]. Two of them — presented in this paper — were made in the workshops of Corinth, one of the main artistic centres of the Archaic Greece [2]. Considerable development of the Corinthian clay modelling art takes place from the beginning of the 7th century B. C. The majority of finds — figurines, architectural details, round plaques, pinaces, loom weights, artifacts with the relief decoration, models of buildings, small altars etc. — is dated to 7th—6th and early 5th century B. C. In the second half of the 6th century B. C. Corinth became the exporter of terracotta objects to the entire Greek world. Alongside the products, also Corinthian influence cleared its path, so many local terracotta varieties made imitations of the Corinth articles. This full bloom of the terracotta production was caused, among others things, by the abundance of easily attainable excellent quality clay in the environs of Corinth.

---

[1] Concerning the history of the University Collection cf. M. L. Bernhard, *Zabytki archeologiczne Zakładu Archeologii Śródziemnomorskiej Uniwersytetu Jagiellońskiego. Katalog*. Praca zbiorowa pod red. M. L. Bernhard, Warszawa—Kraków 1976 (= *Katalog*), pp. 9—18, esp. p. 14; J. Śliwa, *Zur Geschichte der Antikensammlung an der Jagiellonen-Universität*, [in:] *Zur Geschichte der klassischen Archäologie Jena—Kraków*, Wissenschaftliche Beiträge der Friedrich-Schiller-Universität Jena. Jena 1985, pp. 54—66.

[2] The basic publication concerning Corinthian art in the archaic period remains still H. G. G. Payne, *Necrocorinthia. A Study of Corinthian Art in the Archaic Period*. Oxford 1931; see also K. Wallenstein, *Korinthische Plastik des 7. und 6. Jahrhunderts vor Christus*. Bonn 1971; recently the Corinthian art was also the subject of the Author's dissertation *Korynt jako ośrodek greckiej sztuki archaicznej, ok. 720—500 p.n.e.* (*Corinth as a centre of the Archaic Greek art, ca. 720—500 B. C.*, Ph. D. Diss. Cracow 1986).

Many Corinthian terracotta products could boast of high quality, however, the standard of the mass production was much inferior, which is an amazing fact when compared with magnificent plastic vases (manufactured in Corinth mainly in 620—550 B. C.) in form of sphinxes, crouching human figures, lions, rams etc. [3] However, these vases seem to have exerted no influence upon the terracotta products. Criteria which render possible the discernment of the Corinthian terracottas include, among others, characteristic clay and, generally, careful workmanship. The Corinthian clay extraordinarily delicate in structure, is lightly-coloured, cream or greenish, at times light orange. It either contains no mica or, if so, very little of it [4].

The heyday of terracotta production was connected with the introduction of moulds for impressing the figurines, which enabled their production en masse. The practice of using moulds has reached Greece from the East, through Syria or Cyprus or conceivably through both these territories simultaneously [5]. The earliest mould for the production of terracottas known in Greece comes from Corinth. It is a mould in shape of the female head, apparently modelled upon oriental prototypes, but being of local made, discovered in the Potters' Quarter and dated to the beginning of the 7th century B. C. [6].

At first, the moulds in Corinthian workshops were used for impressing the figurines' heads. The bodies of such figurines could have been made in several ways: 1. entirely hand-modelled, 2. impressed in an individual mould, which resulted in a coarse (unworked) back (if the surplus of clay on sides remained not removed, the relief was obtained), and 3. the wheel-shaped lower part of the body assumed cylindrical form, while the upper one was hand-modelled [7]. On the other hand, figurines obtained wholly from an individual mould were to become widespread not before the later part of the 6th century B. C. and were to be mass-produced in Corinth during all the next century to follow [8]. Among the figurines yielded by a single mould, the terracottas representing standing or seated women as well as recumbent male figures have enjoyed the highest popularity. The two first figurine types are represented in the Cracow collection.

---

[3] About Corinthian plastic vases see: Payne, *Necrocorinthia*, pp. 170—180; J. Ducat, *Les vases plastiques corinthienes*, BCH 87, 1963, pp. 431—458; Wallenstein, *Korinthische Plastik ...*, passim.

[4] A. R. Higgins, *Greek Terracottas*. London 1967 (= Higgins, *GT*), p. 48.

[5] *Ibidem*, p. 25.

[6] A. N. Stillwell, *Corinth XV, Part 1, The Potters' Quarter, The Terracottas*. Princeton 1948, pp. 87—88, No. 1, Pl. 29, 1.

[7] R. J. H. Jenkins, *Terracottas*, [in:] H. G. G. Payne et al., *Perachora, The Sanctuaries of Hera Akraia and Limenia*. Vol. I: *Architecture, Bronzes, Terracottas*. Oxford 1940 (= Jenkins), p. 193.

[8] A. N. Stillwell, *Corinth XV, Part 2, The Potters' Quarter, The Terracottas*. Princeton 1952 (= Stillwell), p. 10.

Pl. I. Standing woman, Inv. No. 10.015

Pl. II. Seated woman. Inv. No. 10.011

1. Standing woman (Pl. I)

The figurine shows the woman standing on a low rectangular base shaped in a mould together with the figurine [9]. The woman is clad in a long chiton featuring the *kolpos* with elongated sides, reaching down the feet. Below the *kolpos*, the chiton clings closely to the legs and at sides it is gathered into small vertical folds. In her right hand, sticking to the bosom, the woman holds a dove (?), whereas in the left hand, placed somewhat lower, has a fruit. Her head is adorned with a high polos, slightly widening upwards. The hair, slipping from beneath the polos drops symmetrically on both sides of the neck upon the shoulders in tiny, horizontally delineated waves, while above the forehead it is arranged curlwise. The face is oval with an eminent forehead, big eyes, straight nose, small mouth, and smallish, round chin. Back of the figurine slightly concave with the traces of smoothing out.

The above described figurine belongs to the large group of terracottas representing standing women, sometimes defined as "korai" [10]. Such a type of terracottas was also made in the Eastern Greece's or Sicilian centres, yet here they had a plastically shaped rear part. On the other hand, the type of standing female figure completely flat on the back, as in the case of the Cracow object in question, is undoubtedly a Corinthian invention [11]. Such figurines were mass-produced in this centre and very widely exported from the end of the 6th century B. C. on and subsequently in the course of the whole 5th century B. C. They appear in the majority of sites having been reached earlier, i. e. in last years of the 7th and in the beginnings of the 6th century B. C., by the Corinthian pottery — in numerous sites of both mainland and insular Greece, in southern Italy and Sicily, in Cyrenaica, in the land of Albania and in southern regions of the USSR [12]. Most often however, the type of the standing *kora* is to be encountered right in Corinth and in the Corinthia region, including Perachora. The figurines coming from Heraion in Perachora have been divided by R. J. H. Jenkins into several groups [13].

The Cracow figurine discussed here has been included by K. Moczulska [14] into the type F in the Jenkins' classification [15]. In that type *kolpos*

---

[9] Inv. No. 10.015, H. 0.113 m; buff cream clay, head and shoulders broken off, now glued together, the surface of the figurine effaced. First published by K. Moczulska, [in:] *Katalog*, p. 127, No. 226 (without illustration).

[10] On class of standing women cf. Payne, *Necrocorinthia*, p. 245, note 3, type I—III; Jenkins, p. 218 ff., LC IV type A—D, F; Knoblauch, *Studien zur archaisch-griechischen Tonbildnerei*. Bleicherode am Harz 1937, p. 219 ff., type C; Stillwell, Class X, pp. 84—94, Pls. 14—16.

[11] Stillwell, pp. 13 f. and 84 f.

[12] Higgins, *GT*, p. 85.

[13] Jenkins, as above (see note 10).

[14] Moczulska, as above (see note 9).

[15] Jenkins, p. 219, Nos. 100 and 101, Pl. 95.

and the lower part of chiton have the folds regularly distributed in the whole front part of the figurine. Since the Cracow object displays a triple disposition of creases in the lower part of chiton (groups of creases between the legs and on sides), it should be classified with the Jenkins' type C [16]. This group is distinguished, apart from the described manner of representing the garment, also by the lack of himation. The dating of both groups is uncertain. Jenkins has determined the development time of the group C to the years 530—500 B. C. and that of the group F to years 500—480 B. C., having based himself on comparison of the ways of the garment rendering in contemporary red-figured painting. However, Jenkins himself stresses that the *korai* of type C continued to be manufactured as before in the 5th century B. C. [17] This fact is corroborated by the finds in the Potters' Quarter in Corinth. According to A. N. Stillwell, all the well-made figurines of standing women from the Potters' Quarter, i. e. those which seem to stand closer to the style of the end of the 6th century B. C., have their central and side folds marked in the lower part of chiton. Yet, the earliest dating of the type with the central fold may relate to the most ancient mould, since, as is known, the moulds remained in use for a very long time so that in the 5th century B. C. the figurines were still being produced in the archaic type moulds [18]. A good example, very closely tied to the Cracow figurine, discussed here, is a mould-type of figurine No. 18 from the Potters' Quarter with a triple scheme of creases [19] Eleven figurines have been found impressed in such a type of mould, from which the earliest, coming from the Aphrodite Deposit, is dated to the end of the 6th century B. C. and to the beginning of the 5th century B. C., while the latest from the so-called Circle Deposit comes from the end of the 5th century B. C. Of course, it does not mean that a single mould remained in use for such a long time span, but that a new identical mould was produced after the original one had been worn. In this way, figurines of the given type could have been manufactured even in the course of tens of years.

Reverting to the Cracow figurine, it can be stated that the triple fold scheme in the lower part of chiton alongside careful manner of the hair-do rendering described above say for its early dating within the type C, to which it does belong. A hair rendering in similar way has also one of the earliest korai from the Potters' Quarter, coming from already mentioned Aphrodite Deposit and dated to the end of the 6th century B. C. — beginning of the 5th century B. C. [20] Very closely related to the object

---

[16] *Ibidem*, No. 97, Pl. 95.
[17] *Ibidem*, p. 219.
[18] Stillwell, p. 84 and note 7.
[19] *Ibidem*, p. 91, Pl. 15.
[20] *Ibidem*, p. 88, No. 1 in Class X, Pl. 15.

in question are two figurines of standing women in British Museum [21], dated to 530—500 B. C. Also other figurines representing standing women with folds shown in the central and side parts of chiton bear analogy to the Cracow terracotta; they come from many sites [22], because the type C falls into the rank of types most popular within the whole class of standing women, like the type F in the Jenkins' classification.

To recapitulate, the said object belongs to the type C distinguished by Jenkins from among the category of standing women and could have came into existence in the years 530—500 B. C. However, considering the long employment of moulds of the same type, its dating to the 5th century B. C. cannot be excluded.

2. Seated woman (Pl. II)

The figurine shows the woman seated frontally on a high-back chair with the "leaves" protruding on sides [23]. The woman is clad in a garment reaching down the feet reposing on a low footstool. In the left hand clinging to the breast, she holds a dove, while the right hand reclines on a knee. The face, of a triangular outline, is somewhat blurred, hair arranged in curls above

---

[21] A. R. Higgins, *Catalogue of the Terracottas in the Department of Greek and Roman Antiquities, British Museum.* Vol. I. London 1954, p. 246, Nos. 904 and 905, Pl. 131.

[22] Cf. R. G. Richardson, *Figurines from Corinth*, AJA 2, 1898, p. 212, Fig. 18; D. M. Robinson, *Ointment Vases from Corinth*, AJA 10, 1906, pp. 165—166, Pl. XI, 15; C. Waldstein, *The Argive Heraeum*. Vol. 2. Boston—New York 1902—1905, p. 34, No. 166, Pl. 46,9 and No. 172, Pl. 46,4; C. Blinkenberg, *Lindos, fouilles et recherches*. Vol. I. Berlin 1931, p. 527 f., Nos. 2180—2182, Pl. 100; K. A. Rhomaios, Κόραι τῆς Αἰτωχίας, Deltion 6, 1920—21, p. 70, Fig. 4 (middle) and p. 71, Fig. 5, from temple near Thermos; P. Orsi, *Sicilia*, NsC 2, 1905, p. 440, Fig. 23 (first from right); Ph. E. Legrand, *Antiquités de Tresène*, BCH 29, 1905, p. 307, Fig. 25; D. G. Hogharth, *Excavations at Naucratis*, BSA 5, 1898—1899, p. 81, No. 24; R. J. H. Jenkins, *Researches at Isthmia*, BSA 32, 1931—32, pp. 87—88, Fig. 12 a (dated ca. 500 B. C.); G. Welter, *Troizen und Kalaureia*. Berlin 1941, p. 22, Pl. 9b, Nos. 8 and 9 (local products based an Corinthian types); S. Papaspiridi-Karouzou, Ἀνασκαφή ταφων τοῦ Ἀργους, Deltion 15, 1933—1935, Pl. 2 (first from left); Heurtley, M. Robinson, *Excavations in Ithaca, V: The Geometric and later finds from Aetos*, BSA 43, 1948, p. 113, No. A 3; L. Quarles van Ufford, *Les terres-cuites Siciliennes*. Assen 1941, Fig. 29 (from Megara Hyblaea); D. M. Robinson, *Excavations at Olynthus*. Vol. XIV. Baltimore 1952, pp. 153—156, Nos. 183 and 184, Pl. 60; G. R. Davidson, *Corinth XII, The Minor Objects*. Princeton 1952, p. 30, No. 97, Pl. 7; E. G. Pemberton, *The Vrysoula Classical Deposit from Ancient Corinth*, Hesperia 39, 1970, p. 303, No. 158, Pl. 75; P. G. Themelis, Δελφοί καί περιοχή τον 8. καί 7. π.χ. αἰώνα, ASAtene 61, 1983, p. 245, Fig. 46 (first from right) and p. 241; figurines of this type were also found in sanctuary of Demeter and Kore on Acrocorinth (unpublished).

[23] Inv. No. 10.011, H. 0.089 m; yellow clay, face and polos slightly injured, the surface of torso effaced, traces of red paint are visible on polos and on the sides of the chair. First published by K. Moczulska, [in:] *Katalog*, p. 125, No. 222 (without illustration).

the low forehead sinks symmetrically on both sides of the neck down the shoulders in tiny, horizontally delineated waves. The head is adorned by *polos*. Knife incisions on the back and the bottom. There is the regular hollow on the back of the figurine.

The Cracow terracotta represents another, apart from that of the standing woman, type of a figurine impressed in an individual mould, popular with the Corinthian artisans [24]. As in the former case, we deal here with a type originating probably from the 6th century B. C., but being manufactured, as proved by the finds from the Potters' Quarter in Corinth, in an unaltered form in the 5th and 4th century B. C. [25] The figurines of seated women were also produced in other centres [26], but the Corinth type displays specific features making its identification possible. Here come as follows, a solidly-looking chair, as if made of a single block and without the arm-rests, stiff, frontal attitude of the figurine, the garment resembling tight dress, presence of *polos* and fact of only the figurine's forepart being impressed in a mould [27]. Such terracottas (sometimes made of a local clay) are being found in various sites besides Corinth (mainly in the mainland Greece and Egina), but had never enjoyed such a popularity neither been so widespread as the standing *korai* type [28].

The object discussed here, coming from the Jagellonian University collection, has its numerous counterparts [29], but it bears the closest resemblance to an almost identical statuette from Perachora [30]. The later places itself within the type A, distinguished by Jenkins in the class of terracottas representing seated woman, and dates back to the last quarter of the 6th century B. C. [31] Therefore, the Cracow figurine can also be classified with the type A and similarly dated. However it should be kept

---

[24] On class of seated women see: Payne, *Necrocorinthia*, p. 245, note 3, type IV; Jenkins, p. 220, LC. IV; Stillwell, pp. 94—97, Class XI, Pl. 17.

[25] Stillwell, p. 95.

[26] For example in Attica: Higgins, *GT*, Pl. 72, Pl. 29, p. 74, Fig. 24, Pl. 30 C; in Rhodes: Higgins, *GT*, p. 35, Pl. 13 A—B, p. 63, Pl. 24 B, and in other sites.

[27] Stillwell, p. 95.

[28] *Ibidem*, pp. 14 and 96.

[29] Cf. Richardson, *Figurines* ..., p. 214, Figs. 19 and 20; F. Winter, *Die Typen der figürlichen Terrakotten I* (Die antiken Terrakotten III). Berlin—Stuttgart 1903, p. 50, No. 7; Waldstein, *The Argive Heraeum 2*, p. 36, No. 199, Pl. 46,15; Rhomaios, *Κόραι* ..., p. 74 f., No. 38, Figs. 7,4 and 39; D. M. Robinson, *Excavations at Olynthus IV*. Baltimore 1931, p. 39 f., No. 255, Pl. 23; idem, *Excavations at Olynthus VII*. Baltimore 1933, p. 66, No. 247, Pl. 30; idem, *Excavations at Olynthus XIV*, p. 123 f., No. 140, Pl. 53; G. Daux, *Chronique de fouilles*, BCH 91, 1967, p. 644, Fig. 1 (from Pitsa near Corinth); Davidson, *Corinth XII*, p. 32, Nos. 118 and 119, Pl. 8; C. Roebuck, *Corinth XIV, The Asklepieion and Lerna*. Princeton 1951, p. 130, No. 5, Pl. 52,5; others from Corinth, also from Sanctuary of Demeter and Kore on Acrocorinth (unpublished).

[30] Jenkins, pp. 211—220, No. 102, Pl. 96.

[31] *Ibidem*, pp. 219—221, among the figurines of seated women found at Perachora distinguished four types (A—D).

in mind that reservations concerning the dating of figurines representing seated women must be taken into consideration as well, since the discussed terracotta type was also impressed in a mould which could have remained in use for a long time.

The figurines analogical to the type A from Perachora were also found in the Potters' Quarter in Corinth [32]. The Cracow terracota described above differs from the mentioned figurines from Perachora and Corinth with regard to the manner of rendering the hair, particularly above the forehead, where it is arranged in looks, while those figurines have the hair parted and sinking to the sides in slightly undulated strands. A coiffure similar to that of the discussed Cracow object is to be found in a figurine of a seated woman in British Museum, dated to the beginning of the 5th century B. C., though the later represents different type [33].

In the light of the above considerations, the Cracow object finds its place within the type A of seated women in the Jenkins' classification and could have originated in the Corinth workshops in the last quarter of the 6th or in the beginning of the 5th century B. C.

---

[32] Stillwell, p. 96, Nos. 1—3, Pl. 17.
[33] Higgins, *Catalogue of Terracottas* ..., p. 247, No. 908, Pl. 131.

Verena Paul-Zinserling
Jena

BEGIERDE UND SYMPLEGMA
Zu zwei Schalen des Q- und des Jena-Malers

Für das Innenbild einer rotfigurigen Schale mit niedrigem Fuß in Wien (Abb. 1) hatte F. Eichler [1] noch den Jena-Maler selbst in Betracht gezogen, Beazley [2] schrieb es dem Q-Maler zu. Doch bleibt die von Eichler hervorgehobene enge Verwandschaft zur Würzburger Schale L 492 des Jena-Malers [3] stilistisch und inhaltlich unbestreitbar. Beide Schaleninnenbilder führen auf das Gebiet dionysischer Sexualität, d. h. allgemein der Sexualität in der Spätklassik.

Im Tondo der Wiener Schale nähert sich ein ithyphallischer kranzgeschmuckter Satyr, Eichler nannte ihn Silen, einer nackten, auf einem Felsensitz eingeschlafenen Mänade, um sie aufzuwecken bzw. zu überwältigen. Beide Gestalten sind, bedingt durch das Schalenrund, dicht zusammengestellt, die Beine überschneiden sich, und die begehrlich ausgestreckte Rechte des Satyrn hat den Körper der Schlafenden, die den Kopf auf die linke Schulter stützt, schon erreicht.

Das Motiv der schlafenden Mänade, der sich lüsterne Satyrn nähern, ist in der attischen Vasenmalerei seit dem 3. Viertel des 6. Jh., vor allem dem Frührotfigurigen [4] gut bekannt [5] und fand in der schlafenden Ariadne,

---

[1] *CVA* Wien, Kunsthist. Mus. 1 (1951) 24, Taf. 26, 1—4.

[2] Beazley, *ARV²*, 1519, 15.

[3] Vgl. E. Langlotz, *Griechische Vasen in Würzburg*. München 1936, Taf. 162 f.; A. Rumpf, *Parrhasios*, AJA 55, 1951, 11 und Anm. 77; Beazley, *ARV²*, 1512, 18; Beazley, *Paralipomena*, 499, 18; H. Froning, *Herakles und Dionysos auf einer Schale des 4. Jh. v. Chr. in Würzburg*, WürzbJbAWiss N. F. I 1975, FS. E. Siegmann, 202 Anm. 6; Keuls, *Reign*, 365, Abb. 304.

[4] Erste rf. Fassung des Motivs: Schale des Epidromos-Malers, Berlin—West, Antikenmus. 3232: L. D. Caskey, J. D. Beazley, *Attic Vase Paintings in the Mus. of Fine Arts Boston II*. Oxford 1954, 96 Nr. 4; Beazley, *ARV²*, 117, 2; *CVA* Berlin, Antiquarium 2 (1962), Taf. 63.

[5] Vgl. dazu Caskey, Beazley (wie Anm. 4), 95—99; außerdem Schale Mainz, Universität 104: R. Hampe, E. Simon, *Griechisches Leben im Spiegel der Kunst*. Mainz

die von den Satyrn des Gottes aufgefunden wird, eine enge Parallele, so daß die Entscheidung, ob Ariadne oder eine Mänade in der Schlafenden zu erkennen sei, von den Gelehrten — wie im Fall einer Pelike in London — unterschiedlich getroffen werden konnte [6]. Dennoch gehören die im verwandten Bildschema gestalteten Szenen in verschiedene Themenkreise: Ariadne wird geweckt, um in den Thiasos ihres göttlichen Bräutigams aufgenommen zu werden, für die Mänade ist der nächste Schritt die so häufig gestaltete vehemente Abwehr der Satyrbegierde oder die Liebesvereinigung wie auf der Schale in Würzburg. Gegenteiliger Ansicht ist E. Keuls [7], die wegen des häufigen Vorkommens des Motivs die Anspielung auf die Dionysosankunft bei der schlafenden Ariadne in Naxos unterlegen will. "When they feel up their sleeping Maenad companions, the satyrs are acting out the first mating of Dionysos with Ariadne". Für sie ist die neue sexuelle Erfahrung Ariadnes der Kern des mythischen Ereignisses. Auch für Ariadne und Dionysos ist ein 'Symplegma' auf einer Leningrader Oinochoe [8] überliefert. Metzger glaubte dieses Vasenbild aus der Traditionslinie des Satyrspiels erklären zu können, obwohl gerade es sich in seiner Zurückhaltung von den derb-erotischen Bildern aus dem dionysischen und nichtdionysischen Bereich abhebt. Im Liebespaar auf der Berliner Kanne des Schuwalow-Malers [9] findet sich ein motivischer Vorläufer. Für unser Schalenbild ist die Mänade unbezweifelt, wenn sie auch namenlos bleibt wie der Satyr, über dessen Kopf Farbkleckse vielleicht an eine Namensbeischrift, wie sie bei diesem Motiv vorkommt (s. u.), erinnern sollten. Der Q-Maler knüpft mit seiner Schale an Gestaltungen an, die etwa eine Generation zurück liegen. Um 430 — 20 sind drei Kannen entstanden, die unser Motiv variieren. Auf der Oinochoe des Hobart-Malers in Oxford [10] schleicht sich der Satyr Kissos — Efeu — an die auf einem mit Pantherfell und Weinlaub belegten Felsensitz zusammen-

---

1959, Taf. 12; Schale des Onesimos, Aleria, Korsika: Beazley, *ARV²* 1615. 1645 f.; Beazley, *Paralipomena* 359,9; J. und L. Jehasse, *La nécropole préromaine d'Aleria 1960—1968*, Gallia Suppl. 25. Paris 1973, Nr. 107, Taf. 23 f.; Schale Hamburg mit dem Gegenbild eines 'städtischen' Silens und einer Hetäre: W. Hornbostel, *Aus Gräbern und Heiligtümern. Die Antikensammlung W. Kropatscheck.* Mainz 1980, 123 ff., Nr. 72; Lukanische Kanne 66/12, Karlsruhe vgl. *Griechische Vasen* (Bildhefte des Badischen Landesmus. Karlsruhe) Karlsruhe 1975, Nr. 64; Keuls, *Reign*, 368 f., Abb. 307—309.

[6] Pelike, London Brit. Mus. 1901.7 — 10.5: Schefold, *UKV* Nr. 515 Taf. 4, 2; Metzger, *Représentations*, 111, Nr. 8, Taf. 10 mit Deutung auf Ariadne. Anders: A. v. Salis, *Zur Neapler Satyrspielvase*, JdI 25, 1910, 137; Caskey, Beazley (wie Anm. 4), 97, Nr. 27. Unter den Gemälden im Dionysos Eleuthereus Tempel nennt Paus. 1, 20, 3 auch eine schlafende Ariadne.

[7] Keuls, *Reign*, 366.

[8] Leningrad, Ermitage St. 2074: Schefold, *KV*, Taf. 4a; Schefold, *UKV*, Nr. 302; Metzger, *Représentations*, 120, Nr. 32, Taf. 13,1; 398.

[9] Berlin, Staatl. Mus. 2414: Beazley, *ARV²*, 1208, 41; 1704; A. Greifenhagen, *Antike Kunstwerke.* Berlin 1966², 49, Taf. 57.

[10] *CVA* Oxford, Ashmolean Mus. (1927) Taf. 43, 2; Beazley, *ARV²*, 1258, 1.

gesunkene Mänade Tragoidia. Dieses Paar wird noch einmal von diesem Maler, diesmal als Familie, auf einer Oinochoe in Florenz/Leipzig [11] zusammengestellt. Etwas früher ist eine Oinochoe in Frankfurt [12] anzusetzen, mit der gleichen Szene. Diesmal nimmt die nur am Oberkörper nackte Frau eine mehr liegende Haltung ein, während der Satyr wie ein springender Athlet die Arme weit nach ihr ausstreckt. Unserer Schale am nächsten aber steht eine Kanne aus dem Kreis des Dinos-Malers in Boston [13], die das dionysische Paar um einen zweiten im Rücken der Schlafenden heranschleichenden Satyrn erweitert zeigt. Das Motiv der schlafenden Mänade, der sich wie auf einem Krater in Würzburg [14] ein knabenhafter Satyr nähert, begegnet auch im Atelier des ebenfalls in den ersten Jahrzehnten des 4. Jh. arbeitenden Meleager-Malers. Hinzu kommt ein weiterer Glockenkrater in Athen. Auch in der Tafelmalerei ist das Thema gestaltet worden. So berichtet Plinius von einem Gemälde des Nikomachos "Bacchae obreptantibus satyris", das allerdings erst nach der Schale des Q-Malers entstanden sein wird, aber von der fortdauernden Beliebtheit des Motivs, das auch mit Pan und Sterblichen variiert worden ist, zeugt [15]. In der neueren Forschung hat man dieses Motiv mit Fraueninitiationsriten in Verbindung gebracht [16]. Auch das Thema der körperlichen Liebe, des vollzogenen Koitus, gehört fest in die dionysische Ikonografie. „Dies ist sicher: die sexuelle Erregung gehört wie der Geschlechtsakt selbst in den dionysischen Zusammenhang". J. Marcade [17] sah in der Erotik einen Teil „des heilkräftigen Antriebes der geheimnisvollen Kräfte der Fruchtbarkeit und der Befruchtung". Die Zahl der derb-erotischen Szenen zwischen Satyrn und Mänaden ist vor allem im Schwarzfigurigen groß, während sie zugunsten der Alltags- und Hetärenbilder und homoerotischen Szenen im 5. Jh. zurückgeht, die im letzten Viertel ebenfalls verschwinden [18].

---

[11] Beazley, ARV², 1258, 2.

[12] Vgl. H. Schaal, *Griechische Vasen aus Frankfurter Sammlungen.* Frankfurt/M. 1923, 73, Taf. 48; ders., StädelJb. II 1922, 21 f.; *CVA* Frankfurt 2 (1968), Taf. 79, 1—2.

[13] Vgl. Caskey, Beazley (wie Anm. 4), 97, Nr. 18; G. v. Hoorn, *Choes and Anthesteria,* Leiden 1951, Nr. 376, Abb. 501; Pfuhl, *MuZ* III 222 Nr. 565.

[14] Würzburg, M. v. Wagner Mus. L 523: Langlotz (wie Anm. 3), Taf. 192; Metzger, *Représentations,* 130, Nr. 43, Taf. 16, 3; Beazley, *ARV²,* 1415, 1.

[15] Glockenkrater Athen, Nat. Mus. 1397 (CC. 1936): Caskey, Beazley (wie Anm. 4), 97, Nr. 26; vgl. 98; Plin. HN, 35, 108; H. Brunn, *Geschichte der griechischen Künstler,* II. Stuttgart 1889, 114.

[16] Leider war mir der Aufsatz von C. Clark Kroeger, in: *Abstracts of the 80th General Meeting of the Archaeological Institute of America 28.—30. 12. 1978,* 45 ff. nicht zugänglich.

[17] J. Marcadé, *Eros Kalos. Studie über die erotischen Darstellungen in der griechischen Kunst.* Genf 1962, 56.

[18] Bei der Vielzahl einschlägiger Objekte kann auf eine erneute Zusammenstellung verzichtet werden. Vgl. allgemein: H. Licht, *Sittengeschichte der Griechen,* I—III. Dresden, Zürich 1925—1928; Marcadé (wie Anm. 17); E. Vermeule, *A Love Scene by „the Panaitios-Painter",* AJA, 71, 1967, 310—314; J. Boardman, E. La Rocca,

"Satyr making love to maenad" (Beazley) zeigt das Innenbild einer Schale des Jena-Malers in Würzburg (Abb. 2). Für die Stellung des Paares wies Langlotz auf einen Chalcedon-Skarabäoid des 4. Jh. [19] hin. Eine ähnliche Haltung des kopulierenden Satyr-Mänadenpaares begegnet jedoch schon auf schwarzfigurigen Gefäßen [20]. Die sexuellen Beziehungen von Satyrn, Nymphen und Mänaden gehören seit alters her in den dionysischen Kosmos. So heißt es schon im homerischen Aphroditehymnus [21], daß sich die Nymphen in Liebe mit den Silenen paarten, und im "Kyklops" des Euripides beklagen die Satyrn auch die lange Enthaltsamkeit von sexuellen Vergnügungen [22]. A. Rumpf [23] hatte auf das Wiederaufleben der Freude an erotischen Darstellungen in der Spätklassik, die in den davorliegenden Jahrzehnten weitgehend unterdrückt war, hingewiesen. Dabei hat erstaunlicherweise zwar die Zahl sexueller Themen und Motive zugenommen, wie ja auch die dionysisch-aphrodisische Bildwelt dominiert, die erotischen Gruppen dionysischer Wesen sind aber beinahe ganz verschwunden. Eine sublimierte Hochzeits- und Jenseitssymbolik hat sie offenbar entbehrlich gemacht. Umso interessanter ist daher das Innenbild der Würzburger Schale, dem — soweit wir sehen — kaum etwas Vergleichbares an die Seite gestellt werden kann. Wie Kissos und Tragoidia auf der Kanne in Oxford hat auch das Liebespaar in Würzburg Namen erhalten. Der Satyr Chorillos, also Tänzer, Tänzerchen, liebt sich mit der sich auf felsiger Unterlage abstützenden Mänade Paidia, deren Name hier wohl am zutreffendsten mit Liebesgetändel übersetzt wird. Ch. Fränkel [24] hatte auf seinen erotischen Charakter hingewiesen, so daß Name und Tun der Paidia, die, bevor sie im Gefolge des Dionysos [25] erschien, zu den Begleiterinnen der Aphrodite [26] gehört hat, im Schalenbild des Jena-Malers in Würzburg vorzüglich übereinstimmen. Neben diesem Verständnis als Bild der personifizierten dionysischen Erotik, als deren bevorzugte Träger das Gefolge

---

Eros in Grecia. Milano 1975; Hornbostel (wie Anm. 5), Nr. 53 (K. Schauenburg); C. Johns, *Sex and Symbol. Erotic Images of Greece and Rome.* London 1982; J. Boardman, *Athenian Red Figure Vases.* London 1983², 219; Sutton, *Interaction,* 72—133.

[19] Langlotz (wie Anm. 3), zu Taf. 162; Furtwängler, AG, III, Taf. 61, Nr. 34; J. D. Beazley, *Lewes House Collection of Ancient Gems.* Oxford 1920, Nr. 63.

[20] Bspw. Caeretaner Hydria, Wien, Marcadé (wie Anm. 17), 38, 39.

[21] H. Hom., h. Ven. 262 f.

[22] E. Cyc. 168 ff.

[23] A. Rumpf, *Malerei und Zeichnung,* HdArch, 6. Lief. München 1953, 117: „Es ist kaum ein Zufall, daß die in der reifarchaischen Zeit so zahlreichen Obszönitäten in den Jahrzehnten der hohen Klassik völlig fehlen. Jetzt in der Lebenszeit des Parrhasios tauchen sie auf Vasen wieder auf."; ders., *Parrhasios,* AJA, 55, 1951, 10.

[24] Vgl. Pl. Lg. 667 E; Ch. Fränkel, *Satyr- und Bakchennamen auf Vasenbildern.* Halle 1912, 63 f., 70; RE 36. Hbd. (1942) s. v. Paidiá 2386 f. (Aly).

[25] Fränkel (wie Anm. 24), 104. 106.

[26] Vgl. D. Metzler, *Eunomia und Aphrodite,* Hephaistos, 2, 1980, 74, der offenbar Paideia-Erziehung mit Paidia-Scherz, Spiel gleichgesetzt hat.

viel mehr als der Gott selbst galt, ist eine engere, mehr spezialisierte Deutung dieses Symplegma möglich. Wie H. Froning [27] deutlich gemacht hat, ist Paidia auch die Verkörperung des Satyrspiels, wie die Beischriften einer Pelike aus dem Umkreis des Pronomos-Malers [28] schließen lassen. Paidia, das Satyrspiel, läßt sich ein mit dem Satyrchoreuten Chorillos, dem Vertreter des Satyrchores, ohne den kein Satyrspiel auskam. Ob das Symplegma auf den allgemein erotischen Gehalt oder auch Inhalt der beliebten Satyrspiele anspielen sollte, ist nach Lage unserer Kenntnis über das antike Satyrspiel [29] nicht zu entscheiden. Zweifellos wird es an Anspielungen so wenig gemangelt haben wie in der Komödie [30], ob aber Koitussimulierungen auf offener Bühne stattgefunden haben, ist zumindest zweifelhaft.

In seinem *Structuralist Approach to Greek Vase Painting* beschäftigte sich H. Hoffmann [31] auch mit dem griechischen Mänaden- und Satyrwesen und bewertete die Vasenbilder, vor allem die schon genannten der mänadischen Abwehr, als Ausdruck eines in der Gesellschaft vorhandenen Misogynismus. Der Satyr sei die mißbilligte Verkörperung natürlicher, d. h. tierischer Sexualität und damit als Antipode zur menschlichen Kultur aufzufassen. Das Wesen des griechischen Mannes sei — nach einem E. Leach-Zitat — "the clean passive monk", und Satyr und Mänade seien die abgelehnten Symbole sexueller Anarchie. Ohne sich hier mit diesem Versuch der gesellschaftlichen Rückkoppelung bestimmter in Mythos und Bildwelt hervortretender Erscheinungen auseinandersetzen zu können, sei nur erinnert an die ins Auge fallende Vorliebe für erotische Themen, vom Symplegma auf der Tonmetope von Thermos [32] bis in den ausgehenden Hellenismus, die doch in erster Linie von dem Interesse, der Bedeutung und der Freude an der Sexualität zeugen. In den geordneten Bahnen des Hetärenwesens und der homosexuellen Prostitution gehörte ein gewisses Maß an sexueller Anarchie zum Leben des griechischen Mannes als Gegenstück zum streng gewahrten Gebot ehelicher Treue für die Frau und harter Verfolgung des Ehebruchs für beide Partner [33]. Die zahlreichen

---

[27] H. Froning, *Dithyrambos und Vasenmalerei in Athen* (Beiträge zur Archäologie 2) Würzburg 1971, 10.

[28] Vgl. Froning (wie Anm. 27), Anm. 30; G. Trias de Arribas, *Ceramicas griegas de la Peninsula Iberica*, Bd. 1, 2. Valencia 1967/68, 182 ff., Nr. 589, Taf. 100 ff.

[29] Vgl. dazu Brommer, *Satyrspiele*, 5 ff.; allgemein: D. F. Sutton, *The Greek Satyr Play*, in: Beiträge zur klassischen Philologie, 90, 1980, 142.

[30] Vgl. bspw. Ar. Pax 894 ff.; Ach. 273 ff.

[31] Hoffmann, *Pursuit* 3 f. zu Taf. V 5—6, dazu: Rez. L. Schneider, Hephaistos 1, 1979, 165—169.

[32] Vgl. Pfuhl, *MuZ.* I 493; Ch. Karusos, *ΑΣΠΙΩΈΝ ΝΕΟΙΣΙΝ*, AM 77, 1962, 127, Anm. 13.

[33] Vgl. W. K. Lacey, *Die Familie im antiken Griechenland*, Mainz 1983, 75, 115 ff. Zur Nichtöffentlichkeit der Sexualität der angesehenen Bürger vgl. Sutton, *Interaction*, 114.

3*

erotischen Themen, Motive und Topoi in beinahe allen Bereichen der griechischen Kunst lassen trotz stets vorhandener entgegengesetzter Tendenzen den Schluß zu, daß die körperliche Liebe als ein positiver Wert empfunden wurde und insofern wohl auch das Leach-Zitat nicht zutreffend ist. V. Jarcho [34] hat auf die immerhin von der erstaunlichen Freizügigkeit auch der Bürgermädchen zeugende Tatsache hingewiesen, daß in mehreren der Lustspiele Menanders die Handlung erst durch eine "während irgendwelcher nächtlicher Lustbarkeiten" vorgekommene Vergewaltigung eines Mädchens (aus gutem Hause) ausgelöst bzw. vorwärtsgebracht wird. Daß es sich dabei nicht um einen Ausnahme- und Bühnenfall gehandelt hat, ergibt sich aus dem rechtfertigenden Hinweis des Moschion in der 'Samia' auf die gleichartige Erfahrung tausender junger Menschen, „d. h. der rein erotische Aspekt in den Beziehungen zwischen den Geschlechtern erhält restlose Anerkennung ..." Ebenfalls nicht ohne Einschränkung wird man Hoffmanns Verständnis der sozialen Bewertung der Positionen beim Geschlechtsakt zustimmen können, die er vom homosexuellen Schema, wo der sozial höher gestellte und aktive Partner 'rear-entry sex' ausführt, auf die heterosexuellen Beziehungen überträgt. Die 'front-facing position', der auch unser Schalenbild zuzurechnen ist, sei als 'effeminate' diskriminiert worden [35]. Soweit die von ihm herangezogenen Aristophanes-stellen [36] aussagekräftig sind, lassen sie m. E. einen derartig weitreichenden Schluß nicht zu, da es sich darin um die Verurteilung ganz anderer Liebespraktiken handelt.

Das Symplegma in Würzburg steht in der dionysischen Bildwelt zu Beginn des 4. Jh. ziemlich isoliert, innerhalb der griechischen Kunst allgemein allerdings nicht. Dies könnte die einzige Begründung sein für Eva Keuls [37] ungewöhnliche Deutung der Symplegma-Schale. Sie hält den Satyr für einen verkleideten Mann, der mit einer Hetäre kopuliert. Von erotischen Gemälden spricht der *Hippolytos* des Euripides [38], Aristophanes schrieb eine Komödie über den *Triphales*, den Mann mit den drei Penes. Eupolis soll in seinen *Baptai* das Privatleben des Alkibiades gegeiselt haben, und Lukian charakterisierte das Stück mit den Worten: und bist nicht rot geworden, dieses Stück zu lesen. Nach Ovid füllten die bloßen Titel erotischer Stücke ein ganzes Buch. Demetrios von Phaleron schrieb einen *Erotikos*, und eine Philainis wurde mit einer Schrift über *Schemata*

---

[34] V. Jarcho, *Pflicht und Genuß in den ehelichen Beziehungen der alten Athener*, in: *Actes du VIe Congrès de la Fédération Internationale des Associations d'Etudes Classiques*. Budapest 1984, II, 367.

[35] Sutton, *Interaction*, 77, Rückenstandkoitus sei aus künstlerischem Aspekt (Vermeiden der Horizontalen) bevorzugt worden, 85 f. gegen Hoffmann, Pursuit 4.

[36] Ar. Eq. 1284 ff.; Pax 885; 1280.

[37] Vgl. Keuls, *Reign*, 362.

[38] E. Hipp. 993.

1. Rotfigurige Schale des Q-Malers, Wien, Kunsthistorisches Museum

2. Rotfigurige Schale des Jena-Malers, Würzburg, Martin v. Wagner-Museum

des Zusammenseins in Verbindung gebracht [39]. Polemon erwähnt bei Athenaios [40] als Pornographoi Pausias, Nikophanes und Aristides, alles führende Maler dieser Zeit [41]. Parrhasios [42] hat in kleineren Bildern 'libidines' gemalt, und besonders berühmt war sein Gemälde 'Meleagro Atalante ore morigeratur'. Vom Sohn des Praxiteles, Kephisodotos [43] kannte man eine Symplegmagruppe.

Auch in der Kleinkunst hat es im 4. Jh. neben Malerei und Skulptur drastische erotische Szenen gegeben wie ein korinthischer Spiegel aus dem 3. Viertel des 4. Jh. in Boston [44] beweist.

Trotz dieser sich nur teilweise auf Athen beziehenden Nachrichten und Denkmäler bleibt das Problem, in welchem Maße das erotische Element in der spätklassischen Kunst ins Gewicht fiel, offen. Dennoch scheint sich hier eine Tendenz abzuzeichnen, die mit der Unterhöhlung der alten Sozialstruktur der Polis durch die expandierende ökonomische Entwicklung, beginnend in der 2. Hälfte des 5. Jh., zusammenhängt, und die nicht nur die starke Schicht der zwar wohlhabenden und unentbehrlichen, aber politisch rechtlosen Nichtbürger hervorbrachte [45], sondern auch zu neuen Formen einer privateren Lebensführung beitrug. Individuelles Luxusbedürfnis und persönlicher Lustgewinn als Forderung der sich den Schranken der Polismoral entziehenden starken Oberschicht, deren skrupelloser Egozentrismus in Platons Gorgias [46] kaum ins Reich philosophischer Fantasie gehören wird, haben nicht nur die Wertschätzung der Bildung, wie sie bei Isokrates [47] spürbar wird, bewirkt, sondern auch an die unterhaltende und anregende Funktion der Künste neue Anforderungen gestellt.

Der Jena-Maler scheint also mit seinem erotischen Symplegma dem Bedürfnis seiner Käufer nach sexueller Attraktion entsprochen zu haben und das Innenbild wird wohl auch in der Vasenmalerei nicht allein gestan,

---

[39] Vgl. Licht I (wie Anm. 18), 128. 188. 213 f.; RE 38. Hbd. (1938) s. v. Philainis 2122 (Maas); RE Suppl. XII (1970) s. v. Aristophanes 1403; 1410 Deutung auf Alkibiades unsicher (Gelzer).

[40] Ath. XIII 567 B.

[41] Zu Pausias vgl. Overbeck, *Schriftquellen* 1762; H. Brunn, *Geschichte der griechischen Künstler*, II, Stuttgart 1889, 103; Nikophanes: Overbeck 1767, Brunn 106; Aristides: Overbeck 1762; Brunn 117; Pfuhl, *MuZ* I 748.

[42] Plin. HN 35, 72 = Overbeck, *Schriftquellen* 1718; Suet. Tib. 44 = Overbeck 1719; Brunn (wie Anm. 41), 69; Karusos (wie Anm. 32), 123 f.

[43] Plin. HN 36, 24 = Overbeck, *Schriftquellen* 1339; Brunn I (wie Anm. 41), 276.

[44] Vgl. W. Züchner, *Griechische Klappspiegel*, 14. Ergh. JdI 1942, 66 Nr. 95; Karusos (wie Anm. 32), 123 Anm. 6; Marcadé (wie Anm. 17), 123, 130.

[45] Vgl. J. Pečirka, *The Crisis of the Polis in the Fourth Century*, Eirene 14, 1976, 20 ff.; E. R. Dodds, *Die Griechen und das Irrationale*, Darmstadt 1966, 103 f.

[46] Pl. Grg. 483 A—484 B.

[47] Isoc. 4, 47—50.

den haben, wie es die jetzige Überlieferungssituation erscheinen läßt [48]. Als Symplegma dionysischer Wesen markiert unsere Würzburger Schale offenbar das Ende eines traditionsreichen Motivs in der Vasenkunst.

Neben der oben vorgeschlagenen konkreten Aussage legt diese Darstellung die Frage nach der Möglichkeit einer allgemeineren Bedeutung im dionysischen Vorstellungskreis nahe. Welche Rolle hat die Sexualität im dionysischen Kultgeschehen, im Leben der Dionysosmysten und in ihren Jenseitsvorstellungen gespielt?

Direkte Schriftzeugnisse, die Auskunft geben könnten, sind nicht vorhanden. Lediglich Anspielungen auf die nie ermüdende Sinnlichkeit der Satyrn und die Vorliebe des Gottes, sich mit 'schwarzäugigen Nymphen' [49] zu lieben, d. h. auf sexuelle Beziehungen, die ganz auf der Ebene des Mythos liegen, lassen sich finden. Die verbürgerlichten Satyrn auf den früh- bis spätklassischen Vasenbildern die in unserem Zusammenhang schon mehrfach angesprochen wurden als Zeugnis für die rituelle Wirksamkeit der Weihe, sind weder ithyphallisch noch nähern sie sich ihren Partnerinnen in begehrlicher Absicht spätarchaischer, d. h. mythischer Satyrn. Die Sexualität scheint weitgehend ausgespart seit die Kultpraxis, die verändernde Kraft der Weihen, Opfer und Gebete ins Aufmerksamkeitsfeld der Künstler gerückt waren und die Konzentration auf die Menschen als Gestalter und Teilhaber des religiösen Lebens eingesetzt hatte. In den Riten der Mysterienweihe und der Festzeremonien, soweit sie bekannt sind, aber auch bei der Oreibasie der Thyiaden von Delphi, an der die athenischen Frauen als Gesandtschaft teilnahmen, oder in den kleinasiatischen Thiasoi gibt es keine greifbaren Hinweise auf sexuelle Elemente. Das muß jedoch nicht gleich auch ihr Nichtvorhandensein bedeuten. Immerhin stand im Zentrum der attischen Anthesterien ein *hieros gamos*, eine *symmeixis* wie Aristoteles [50] sich ausdrückt, die Vermählung des Dionysos mit der ersten Athenerin, der Frau des Archon Basileus, der Basilinna. Es wäre müßig, weiter über das 'Wie' dieser geheiligten geschlechtlichen Vereinigung zu spekulieren, sie fand im Bukoleion statt und war das Mysterium, das die Verbindung des Dionysos mit Athen oder wahrscheinlicher mit den attischen Bakchen stets neu herstellte und gleichzeitig symbolisierte. Der Phallos des Gottes wurde in den ländlichen und den städtischen Dionysien aufgestellt und in der Pompe durch die Stadt getragen, er war Votiv und Symbol im Liknon, ihm kam

---

[48] Vgl. Glockenkrater London, Brit. Mus. F 65 des Dinos-Malers mit homoerotischer Szene: Beazley, *ARV²*, 1154, 35.

[49] Vgl. S. O T 1105 f.

[50] Arist. Ath. 3, 5; vgl. L. Deubner, *Attische Feste.* Berlin 1956², 100 ff.; W. Burkert, *Griechische Religion der archaischen und klassischen Epoche* (*Die Religionen der Menschheit*, Bd. 15). Stuttgart, Berlin, Köln, Mainz 1977, 361 ff.; H. W. Parke, *Festivals of the Athenians.* London 1977, 112.

in der dionysischen Symbolik eine zentrale Rolle zu [51]. Selten tritt Dionysos selbst auch als Liebhaber auf, wie auf der schon erwähnten Kanne Kertscher Stils in Leningrad. Die Hochzeitssymbolik der spätklassischen Vasen schließt in jedem Fall die sexuelle Vereinigung ein, indem sie darauf hinzielt, wie in der griechischen Kunst die Gebärde der Entschleierung und der Griff des Handgelenkes cheira epi karpó, durch den Mann die eheliche Inbesitznahme bedeutete [52]. K. Kerényi [53] hatte aus den Bildern unteritalischer Vasen eine erotische Botschaft herausgelesen, nach der der Tod in der Sphäre der Anthesterien als das große erotische Abenteuer aufgefaßt worden sei, und das Bildprogramm einer Spitzamphora in Gießen veranlaßte ihn zu den Worten: „All das will das Mysterium des Todes so erscheinen lassen, als wäre es das Mysterium eines erhöhten Lebens in einer göttlichen Ehe". Auch H. R. W. Smith [54] erkannte in den apulischen Vasenbildern den Hinweis auf erotisches Glück der dionysischen Paare im Jenseits, und auch die dionysischen Mysten Griechenlands werden sexuelle Freuden im Jenseits erwartet haben. Für die Frauen als potentielle Bräute des Gottes selbst, wie sie auf einigen Vasen erscheinen, könnte vor allem durch die Vorstellung der Liebeshingabe erst der Vollzug der Weihe sinnfällig und erlebbar werden. Kerényi [55] schrieb, allerdings für die spätere Antike: „Die Schrecken des Todes wurden durch die Identifikation des Toten mit Dionysos oder durch den Glauben der liebenden Hingabe der weiblichen Verstorbenen an den Gott überwunden". In den mittels einer kommunikativen Gebärdensprache gestalteten dionysischen Szenen auf den Vasen des 4. Jh. ist immer auch die Bestätigung dionysischer Sexualität als Quelle des Lebens, der Freude und der endgültigen Vereinigung enthalten.

---

[51] Vgl. M. P. Nilsson, *Griechische Feste von religiöser Bedeutung mit Ausschluß der attischen*. Leipzig 1906, 261, 263 ff.

[52] Bspw. die Hera-Zeus-Metope vom Hera-Tempel E in Selinunt, Palermo, Nat. Mus.: E. Langlotz, *Die Kunst der Westgriechen in Sizilien und Unteritalien*. München 1963, Taf. 105—108; G. Neumann, *Gesten und Gebärden in der griechischen Kunst*. Berlin 1965, 59—66; Sutton, *Interaction*, 177.181 traditionelle Hochzeitsgeste und Ausdruck der Männerherrschaft.

[53] K. Kerényi, *Dionysos. Urbild des unzerstörbaren Lebens*. München, Wien 1976, 289 ff., 295.

[54] H. R. W. Smith, *Funerary Symbolism in Apulian Vase-Painting* (ed. J. K. Anderson). Berkeley, Los Angeles, London 1976, 63. 79. 84; so auch H. G. Horn, *Mysteriensymbolik auf dem Kölner Dionysosmosaik*. Bonn 1972, 103.

[55] Kerényi (wie Anm. 53), 295 f.

40

Abkürzungen

Außer den im „Archäologischen Anzeiger" zum Jahrbuch des Deutschen Archäologischen Instituts 1982, 809 ff. und in der Archäologischen Bibliographie verwendeten Abkürzungen werden hier noch folgende gebraucht:

Hoffmann, *Pursuit* — H. Hoffmann, *Sexual and Asexual Pursuit. A Structuralist Approach to Greek Vase-Painting*. Occasional Paper 34 of the RAI. London 1977.

Keuls, *Reign* — E. C. Keuls, *The Reign of the Phallus. Sexual Politics in Ancient Athens*. New York 1985.

Metzger, *Représentations* — H. Metzger, *Les Représentations dans la céramique attique du IVᵉ siècle*. Paris 1951.

Schefold, *KV* — K. Schefold, *Kertscher Vasen*. Berlin—Wilmersdorf 1930.

Schefold, *UKV* — K. Schefold, *Untersuchungen zu den Kertscher Vasen*. Berlin, Leipzig 1934.

Sutton, *Interaction* — R. F. Sutton jr., *The Interaction between Men and Women portrayed on Attic Red-figure Pottery*. Chapel Hill 1981 (Ann Arbor 1985).

Małgorzata Wilkosz
Kraków

KATAXAIPE KAI EYΦPAINOY
Le gobelet en verre avec l'inscription grecque

Dans l'ensemble de récipients antiques en verre de la Collection Czartoryski à Cracovie il y a un gobelet avec l'inscription grecque (fig. 1)[1]. Le gobelet cylindrique, soufflé dans un moule en trois parties, est fait en verre jaune-verdâtre. Le bord du récipient est légèrement evasé vers l'extérieur. Ses parois sont ornées de bas-reliefs horizontaux. L'inscription *KATAXAIPE KAI EYΦPAINOY* constitue la bande centrale de la décoration. Elle est divisée en deux parties par les feuilles verticales de palmier qui cachent les traces du moule. Au-dessus de l'inscription se trouve une frise de quatre feuilles de palmier disposées deux par deux avec les pointes dirigées l'une vers l'autre, ainsi que deux lignes en relief. Les mêmes lignes et l'ornement continu de feuilles schématiques bordent le gobelet en bas. Le fond est plat avec un cercle en relief à la distance de 1 cm du bord.

Le récipient étudié provient de la collection de verres antiques réuni par Władysław Czartoryski. Il a été acquis probablement dans les années 1869—1877. Le gobelet avec l'inscription n'est pas encore recensé dans la liste des antiquités de l'Hôtel Lambert de 1869, bien que la liste comprenne un certain nombre de verres antiques[2]. Il a cependant déjà été noté en 1880 dans *Le Catalogue des Antiquités Etrangères au Musée Czartoryski* sous le numéro 118. Ces antiquités arrivaient peu à peu de Paris depuis 1877[3]. D'après la correspondence de W. Czartoryski avec L. Bent-

---

[1] Musée National à Cracovie, Collection Czartoryski, N° Inv. XI-118; Dimensions: haut. 7,8 cm, diam. sup. 7,2 cm; État de conservation: manque du fragment de l'orifice, nombreuses fissures — en général dans la partie inférieure, la partie supérieure couverte d'une mince couche claire-beige de décomposition (par endroits une légère irisation).

[2] Bibliothèque Czartoryski, Ew. XVII/2342.

[3] De la lettre de L. Bentkowski à W. Czartoryski du 15 XI 1880 on apprend que jusqu'à ce temps le *Catalogue des Antiquités* comprenait 282 positions; Bibliothèque Czartoryski, Ew. 1033, p. 127.

kowski on apprend qu'un colis, de février 1877, contenait entre autres „des boîtes de verres grecques" [4]. Parmi les récipients expédiés alors à Cracovie devait se trouver notre gobelet avec l'inscription, car c'était l'unique envoie de verres dans les années 1877—1880.

Le gobelet de la Collection Czartoryski appartient à la grande famille des verres soufflés dans des moules dépliants en argile, ornés de bas-reliefs et portant des inscriptions grecques. Jusqu'à présent la seule étude sur de tels objets a été présentée par D. B. Harden dans ses deux articles de 1935 et 1945 [5]. Parmi plusieurs dizaines de récipients qu'il connaissait il a distingué 11 groupes (A—L) selon le genre des inscriptions qu'ils possédaient. Deux groupes nouveaux (M et N) ont été rajoutés récemment par M. C. McClellan [6].

Le gobelet portant l'inscription *KATAXAIPE KAI EYΦPAINOY* (sois content et amuse-toi) appartient au groupe Fii selon la typologie de D. B. Harden. Celui-ci a distingué deux types parmi les récipients du groupe F [7]. Le premier — Fi avec la forme *KATAIXAIPE* et le deuxième — Fii avec l'orthographe plus correcte *KATAXAIPE*. Ces deux types varient aussi par la graphie de la lettre „alpha". Dans le type Fii la forme est plus ancienne — A; dans Fi plus moderne — Λ, utilisée dans les inscriptions à partir de la période hellénistique. Les fonds des récipients sont aussi exécutés de façon différente. Le gobelet du type Fi possède sur le fond trois cercles concentriques en relief; Fii — seulement un, à la distance de 1 cm du bord, ainsi qu'une petite cavité au centre (ce dernier caractère n'existe pas dans le gobelet de Cracovie).

De plus D. B. Harden a distingué dans le groupe F les objets de type Fx, pour lesquelles on ne peut déterminer l'orthographe de l'inscription en raison de leur état très fragmenté ou des données insuffisantes des publications.

Une exception intéressante dans ce groupe est le récipient du Musée Haaretz à Tel-Aviv, appelé par M. C. McClellan type Fiii [8]. Il se distingue du type Fii que par la bande supérieure de décoration, qui au lieu de quatre feuilles de palmier, typiques pour le groupe F, possède une frise en spirale.

Actuellement nous connaissons 35 gobelets en verre appartenant

---

[4] Bibliothèque Czartoryski, Ew. 2087, lettre N° 190.

[5] D. B. Harden, *Romano-Syrian glasses with mould-blown inscriptions*, Journal of Roman Studies, XXV, 1935, p. 163—186, pl. XXIII—XXVIII; idem, *Two tombs-groups of the first century AD from Yahmour, Syria; and a supplement to the list of roman-syrian glasses with mould-blown inscriptions*, Syria, XXIV, 1944/45, p. 83—95, pl. V—IX.

[6] M. C. McClellan, *Recent finds from Greece of the first century AD mould-blown glass*, Journal of Glass Studies, 25, 1983, p. 71—78.

[7] Harden, *Romano-Syrian glasses* ..., p. 171.

[8] Y. Israeli, *Sidonian mould-blown glass vessels in the Museum Haaretz*, Journal of Glass Studies, 6, 1964, p. 35—36, N° 2, fig. 4; McClellan, *Recent finds* ..., p. 77.

Fig. 1. Le gobelet en verre du Musée National à Cracovie (Collection Czartoryski)

au groupe F: 17 qui représentent le type Fi, 10 — Fii, 1 — Fiii et 7 — Fx.

Il semble peu vraisemblable que D. B. Harden ait connu le gobelet de Cracovie et qu'il l'ait placé dans son catalogue. Seuls deux récipients non localisés, cités par lui dans l'ensemble Fx, pourraient y figurer [9]. Néanmoins dans les deux cas l'état de conservation de ces objets ainsi que les dates des publications excluent leur identification avec le récipient de Cracovie, que W. Czartoryski possédait depuis 1877. Ainsi le gobelet avec l'inscription de la Collection Czartoryski est désormais le onzième objet du type Fii selon la typologie de D. B. Harden.

Dès 35 récipients qui représentent le groupe F, seul un petit nombre fournit des informations permettant la datation de l'ensemble. Parmi les dix objets connus du type Fii, type identique au récipient de la Collection Czartoryski, il faut distinguer surtout deux gobelets trouvés dans les tombes romaines à Yahmour en Syrie. Ayant pour base la forme des autres récipients en verre qui constituaient le mobilier funéraire, D. B. Harden a daté cette trouvaille de la deuxième moitié du Ier siècle [10]. Le gobelet du type Fi trouvé dans la tombe de la nécropole romaine à Siphnos est du dernier quart du Ier siècle. Ces tombes ont été datées à l'aide de derniers de Vespasien et Titus trouvés alentour [11]. De plus — les trouvailles faites au camp romain à Vindonissa confirment la datation des récipients du groupe F pour le Ier siècle. On y a trouvé deux petits fragments d'un gobelet cylindrique avec l'inscription (type Fx) [12].

D. B. Harden avait évalué aproximativement l'époque de production de la famille des récipients à inscriptions aux Ier et IIème siècle [13]. Les recherches archéologiques des dernières années ont fourni les nouvelles données qui permettent de rendre plus précise cette datation. Deux fragments d'un gobelet du groupe A trouvés avec la monnaie de Caligula (37—41 après J. C.) proviennent de Corinthe [14]. Les fouilles à Cosa en Italie effectuées derrière la basilique à côté de forum ont fourni un grand ensemble de verres, datant certainement d'un peu avant 40—45 après J. C. Parmi ces vestiges se trouvait aussi un petit fragment d'un gobelet cylindrique du groupe E [15].

[9] Harden, *Romano-Syrian glasses* ..., p. 173, Fxa et Fxb.

[10] Harden, *Two tombs-groups* ..., p. 82, 84, 86.

[11] J. K. Brock, G. Mackworth Young, *Excavations in Siphnos. IV — The Roman graves of the first century AD*, The Annual of the British School at Athens, 44, 1949, p. 81, 85 N° 5.

[12] L. Berger, *Römische Gläser aus Vindonissa*. Basel 1960, p. 49—50, pl. 8 (N° 117 et 118).

[13] Harden, *Romano-Syrian glasses* ..., p. 181—182.

[14] McClellan, *Recent finds* ..., p. 73.

[15] D. Grose, *Roman glass of the first century AD. A dated deposit of glassware from Cosa, Italy*; Annales du 6e Congrès de AIHV (Cologne 1973), Liège 1974, p. 32—33, 37—38, fig. 1—8, 2; McClellan, *Recent finds* ..., p. 76.

Les fragments de Corinthe et Cosa sont actuellement les plus anciens
exemples de récipients avec inscriptions et permettent de situer le début
de leur production dans le deuxième quart du Ier siècle. Pourtant ils
n'aident pas à déterminer la durée de production de ces récipients dans
les ateliers des verriers. D'après M. C. McClellan, prenant en considération
l'unité intérieure du groupe entier, il est douteux qu'ils aient été produits
par plus d'une ou deux générations d'artisans [16]. On peut donc admettre
que la production des récipients avec inscriptions a lieu dans les limites
du Ier siècle.

Les récipients de ce genre étaient produits sur le bord de la Mer
Méditerranée — probablement dans les ateliers syriens. On les trouve
souvent en Syrie et en Palestine, mais c'est Chypre qui en a fourni le plus
grand nombre. Par exemple, de 21 objets du groupe F, dont la provenance
est déterminée, le plus grand nombre (11 pièces) a été trouvé à Chypre;
pour les autres — trois en Syrie, trois en Italie et en Palestine, Grèce,
Suisse et Crimée — un. Malgré les nombreuses trouvailles à Chypre
B. D. Harden est décidement contre la supposition que la production des
récipients avec inscriptions pouvait y avoir lieu. D'après lui il est
indiscutable que c'est la Syrie qui était le centre de leur production [17].
Dans les sources anciennes Chypre n'a jamais été cité comme lieu de
production de verre et les fouilles archéologiques n'en fournissent aucune
preuve [18]. D'ailleurs les verriers syriens étaient connus dans tout le monde
antique. C'est à eux — selon Pline — qu'était attribuée l'invention du
verre [19]. Les recherches archéologiques confirment aussi la position parti-
culière de la Syrie pour la production des verres dans l'antiquité. Pendant
les premiers siècles après J. C. la Syrie, et spécialement Sidon, était le centre
de la production en série des récipients soufflés dans un moule, ornés en
relief ou bien prenant différentes formes (p. ex. flacons en forme de double
tête, de grappe de raisin, de datte). Les récipients susmentionnés avec les
inscriptions entrent dans cette tradition syrienne de production des verres
avec un riche décor plastique.

En revenant au gobelet avec l'inscription *KATAXAIPE KAI
EYΦPAINOY* de la Collection Czartoryski il faut dire que cet objet est
lié à une grande famille de récipients soufflés dans un moule, portant les
inscriptions grecques, produits au Ier siècle dans les ateliers syriens. Le
récipient de Cracovie est un onzième et nouvel objet dans l'ensemble
de gobelets du type Fii selon la typologie de D. B. Harden.

---

[16] McClellan, *Recent finds* ..., p. 75.
[17] Harden, *Romano-Syrian glasses* ..., p. 181.
[18] O. Vessberg, A. Westholm, *The Swedish Cyprus Expedition*, vol. IV, 3. Lund
1956, p. 194.
[19] Plinius, *Historia Naturalis*, XXXVI, 190.

Ernst Kluwe
Jena

MÜNZEN ALS HISTORISCHE UND KULTURGESCHICHTLICHE ZEUGNISSE
Zur Nutzung der Jenaer Münzsammlungen für wissenschaftliche Studien sowie für Lehrzwecke

Zu den archäologischen Sammlungen der Sektion Altertumswissenschaften der Friedrich-Schiller-Universität Jena gehören auch umfangreiche Münzbestände. Diese setzen sich aus vier einst selbständigen Kollektionen zusammen: der ostasiatischen, der orientalischen, der Sammlung F. W. Schmidt und der „sektionseigenen", die als kleinste mit etwa 300 Exponaten nur „ergänzenden" Charakter hat und im qualitativen Anspruch gegenüber den anderen Sammlungen zurückbleibt. Im Ergebnis kontinuierlicher konservatorischer Arbeiten im letzten Jahrzehnt befinden sich alle Sammlungen in einem ausgezeichneten Erhaltungszustand.

Die ostasiatische und die orientalische Münzsammlung — 7489 Exemplare — ehemals Großherzoglich-orientalische Münzsammlung — kamen erst vor etwa drei Jahrzehnten in die klassisch-archäologischen Sammlungskomplexe. Vor der Überführung wurden sie in den Räumen der Universitätsbibliothek aufbewahrt. Beide Kollektionen sind ungeordnet und wissenschaftlich im wesentlichen unbearbeitet. Um ihren gegenwärtigen Bestand zu sichern und weitere Verluste zu vermeiden, lag das Schwergewicht des Interesses vornehmlich auf konservatorischem Gebiet.

In vielfältiger Form wird hingegen mit den antiken Münzen wissenschaftlich gearbeitet. Den Kern des Bestandes an antiken griechischen und römischen Münzen bildet die Münzsammlung W. H. Schmidt[1]. Sie wurde, wie im Vorwort des gedruckten Kataloges von 1890 hervorgehoben

---

[1] *Verzeichnis der Oberstlieutnant F. W. Schmidt'schen antiken Münzsammlung des Wilhelm-Ernst-Gymnasiums nach der Handschrift des Majors a.D. E. G. Schmidt*, hrsg. von O. Knott. Weimar 1890.

wird, vom „Königlichen Oberstlieutnant und Abteilungschef im Großen Generalstabe Friedrich Wilhelm Schmidt mit Eifer und Umsicht angelegt". Nach dessem Tode 1845 ging sie in den Besitz seines Bruders über, des preußischen Majors Ernst Gottlob Schmidt. Als dieser 1877 verstarb, vermachte er die Münzsammlung dem Großherzoglichen Gymnasium zu Weimar, da sowohl sein Bruder als auch er selbst Schüler dieser Bildungsstätte gewesen waren. Vom Weimarer Gymnasium gelangte die Kollektion in den Besitz des Schloßmuseums Weimar, das sie zur besseren Nutzung und wissenschaftlichen Bearbeitung als Dauerleihgabe dem Archäologischen Institut der Jenaer Universität zur Verfügung stellte. Abgesehen von den Jahren unmittelbar nach dem 2. Weltkrieg, als die Sammlung im Münzkabinett der Staatlichen Museen zu Berlin aufbewahrt und betreut wurde, hat sie so seit Jahrzehnten im wissenschaftlichen Leben — vor allem in der Ausbildung, akademischen Qualifikation [2] sowie populärwissenschaftlichen Publikation und Vortragstätigkeit — der altertumswissenschaftlichen Disziplinen der Friedrich-Schiller-Universität eine wichtige Rolle gespielt und spielt sie auch noch heute.

Aus diesem knappen Abriß der Geschichte der Schmidt'schen Münzsammlung wird bereits ihre Besonderheit deutlich: Es handelt sich um eine Sammlung, die in der ersten Hälfte des 19. Jahrhunderts zusammengetragen und nach dem Tode des Sammlers weder erweitert noch in der Struktur verändert wurde. Der 1890 von dem Weimarer Gymnasiallehrer Otto Knott nach dem handschriftlichen Verzeichnis von Ernst Gottlob Schmidt erarbeitete und gedruckte Katalog enthält die Beschreibungen der Münzbilder und Münzlegenden von 4346 Stücken. Bei der Rückführung der Sammlung in die Kleinkunstsammlung des ehemaligen Archäologischen Instituts der Friedrich-Schiller-Universität im Jahre 1961 waren davon noch 4089 Münzen vorhanden. Von diesen wiederum ließen sich 95 Stücke aussondern, die die wissenschaftliche Bearbeitung bisher eindeutig als Fälschungen erwiesen hatte. Hinzukommen mehr als 20 kunsthistorisch interessante Fälschungen, Paduaner und Beckerfälschungen [3].

---

[2] Diplomarbeiten: P. Arnold, *Barbarendarstellungen auf römischen Reichsmünzen von Augustus bis Diocletian.* Jena 1958; V. Enderlein, *Münzen der Sassanidenzeit.* Jena 1958; U. Türich, *Die Familienangehörigen des Kaisers Augustus auf den römischen Reichsmünzen.* Jena 1984.

[3] Hofrat Karl Wilhelm Becker (1771—1837) gehörte in den Jahren zwischen 1810 und 1830 zu den markantesten Persönlichkeiten des Kunstlebens und des Kunsthandels in Europa sowie als Kenner antiker Münzen. In der Zeit von 1805 bis 1825 muß er über 600 Münzstempel geschnitten haben, ohne daß seine Fälschertätigkeit zunächst erkannt wurde. Erst als die Beckerschen Schöpfungen immer häufiger im Kunsthandel auftauchten, wurde man auf ihn aufmerksam, diskutierte nun sein Verhalten in der Öffentlichkeit, in Zeitungen und Zeitschriften. In der Mitte der 20er Jahre sah sich Becker daher gezwungen, sich als Nachahmer antiker und anderer Münzen erkennen zu geben. Damit verbunden war die Herausgabe eines von Becker gefertigten Verzeichnisses der Münzen, die er „zu seinem Vergnügen" geschaffen hatte. Zu einigen Fälschungen der Jenaer

Zu den 4089 vorhandenen Stücken des Kataloges von 1890 kommen 224 Münzen, die in den Jahrzehnten zwischen 1890 und 1960 durch "zielgerichtete" Vertauschungen in die Sammlung gelangten. Meistens handelt es sich um schlecht erhaltene Stücke.

In der Mehrzahl von mäßiger Qualität sind auch die Exponate der „sektionseigenen" Sammlung, zudem anscheinend allein nach dem Zufälligkeitsprinzip des Schenkens zusammengekommen. Eine Untersuchung zur Entstehungsgeschichte dieser Kollektion anhand der Archivbestände der Jenaer Universität [4] steht noch aus.

Der Anteil der griechischen Münzen am Gesamtbestand der antiken Prägungen ist nur klein — etwa ein Fünfzigstel. Zudem handelt es sich meistens um abgegriffene Aes-Stücke des 4. Jh. v. u. Z., vor allem aber der hellenistischen Periode. Besser erhalten sind durchweg die wenigen Silbermünzen. Sie vermitteln insbesondere eine Vorstellung von griechischer Münzkunst und deren ästhetischen Wertmaßstäben, auch wenn es sich bei diesen attraktiven Exponaten um bekannte und verbreitete Typen handelt (Abb. 1—4).

Zusammengefaßt bietet der Gesamtbestand an Griechenmünzen trotz der gemachten Einschränkungen eine solide Basis, um anhand von Münzoriginalen die Studierenden komplex mit dem Gegenstand und den Methoden antiker griechischer Numismatik vertraut zu machen, theoretische und praktische Ausbildung eng miteinander zu verbinden. Im Mittelpunkt der Lehraktivitäten stehen Zielstellungen, die in der Fachterminologie unter dem Begriff Münzkunde gefaßt werden: Beschreibung, Bestimmung und systematische Ordnung von Münzmaterial. Nur wenige Studierende werden zu der Befähigungsstufe weitergeführt, die die Münzforschung als Qualifizierungsniveau heute voraussetzt, wenn man in der Münze „ein Denkmal mit Aussagen staatlicher, politischer, rechtlicher, religiöser, mythologischer, ästhetischer, paläographischer — überhaupt kultureller Art (H. Gebhart), damit eine staatsrechtliche, speziell kunst-, wirtschafts und religionsgeschichtliche, aber auch allgemein historische Quelle" [5] sieht.

Was mittels der griechischen Münzen angelegt und vermittelt wird, erhält auf der wesentlich breiteren Basis der römisch-republikanischen und römisch-kaiserzeitlichen Prägungen seine Vertiefung.

Der Bestand an römischen Münzen genügt, um in entsprechendem Maße den Anforderungen zu genügen, die an eine Studien- und Lehrsammlung einer Universitätseinrichtung zu stellen sind. Er umfaßt Prägungen

---

Sammlung vgl. E. Kluwe, *Fälschungen antiker Münzen in der Sammlung antiker Kleinkunst der Sektion Altertumswissenschaften der Friedrich-Schiller-Universität Jena*, in: *Reichtümer und Raritäten II.* Jena 1981, 126—137.

[4] In den alten archäologischen Katalogen und Inventaren sowie in dem wenigen vorhandenen Schriftgut wird diese Münzsammlung nicht erwähnt.

[5] K. Christ, *Antike Numismatik.* Darmstadt 1967, 9.

vom späten 3. Jh. v. u. Z. bis in das 6. Jh. u. Z., reicht mit Einzelexemplaren zudem noch weiter in die byzantinische Periode hinein. Wissenschaftlich in ausreichender Form bearbeitet — als in sich geschlossener Komplex — sind nur die Münzen der Sammlung Schmidt. Sie und die sektionseigene Kollektion ergänzen sich insofern, als die Sammlung Schmidt nur römische Reichsmünzen enthält, die sektionseigene hingegen eine große Zahl von kaiserzeitlichen Provinzialprägungen. Beide Kollektionen können eine Reihe von künstlerisch herausragenden und historisch interessanten Prägungen vorweisen. Einige dieser Stücke sollen im folgenden vorgestellt werden.

Bekannterweise trat Rom erst verhältnismäßig spät in den Kreis der eigenes Münzgeld herausgebenden Mächte ein. Die Vorgeldformen (Aes rude und Aes signatum) sowie das frühe Kupfergeld (Aes grave — Schwergeld) sind in der Jenaer Sammlung nicht mit Beispielen vertreten. Die vorhandenen Kupfermünzen (Abb. 5) gehören bereits ins 2. Jh. v. u. Z., als infolge ständiger Gewichtsreduzierung auch das Kupfergeld handliche Formen angenommen hatte.

Im 3. Jh. v. u. Z. begann der römische Staat sein Geldwesen konsequenter unter Kontrolle zu nehmen und zu entwickeln. Das jährlich neu besetzte Amt der *tresviri monetales* wurde eingeführt und dieses Dreimännerkollegium für das Ausschmelzen und Prägen von Bronze, Silber sowie Gold verantwortlich gemacht. Um den wachsenden Erfordernissen der Außen- und Militärpolitik entsprechen zu können, begann man in Campanien Silbermünzen prägen zu lassen. Als Vorbilder dienten die Prägungen der Griechen, deren Währungssystem im 3. Jh. v. u. Z. noch völlig dominierte. Didrachmen (Abb. 6), Quadrigaten (Abb. 6) und Victoriaten wurden zunächst in Campanien, dann in Rom selbst herausgegeben. Auf den Prägeherren weist nur die Legende hin — Romano (für Romanom, später Roma).

Am Ende des 3. Jh. v. u. Z. (211 v. u. Z.) entstand dann jenes römische Münznominal, das für Jahrhunderte zum Standard werden sollte — der Denar [6]. Er war auf das Bronzeas bezogen, wog 4,55 g und hatte einen Wert von 10 Assen (daher Wertzeichen X). Als Münzbilder (Abb. 7) zeigt der Denar auf seiner Vorderseite den behelmten Kopf der Stadtgöttin Roma, auf seiner Rückseite die Dioskuren, die Zwillinge Kastor und Pollux zu Pferde. Später kommen als Rückseitenbilder Biga- (Abb. 8) und Quadrigadarstellungen (Abb. 9) hinzu. Bis zur Mitte des 2. Jh. v. u. Z. beherrschen gleichbleibende Münzbilder die Szenerie, ein klarer Ausweis dafür, daß der römische Staat in der Phase seiner forcierten Expansionspolitik mit ihren Krisenperioden auf dem Gebiet des Münzwesens stets als geschlossene Einheit auftrat.

---

[6] Der Denar war während der späten Republik die Hauptmünze. Als Rechnungseinheit fungierte indes der Sesterz, der in dieser Zeit allerdings nur selten ausgeprägt wurde (= 2 1/2 Asse).

TAFEL I

1

a
b

2

a
b

3

a
b

4

a
b

TAFEL II

5
a
b

6
a
b

7
a
b

8
a
b

9
a
b

TAFEL III

10

a   b

11

a   b

12

a   b

13

a   b

14

a   b

15

a   b

16

a   b

17

a   b

Mit der Eroberung der hellenistischen Staatenwelt begann sich die Situation grundlegend zu verändern. Die selbständige griechische Münzprägung kam zum Erliegen, die römische beherrschte von nun an allein den Markt; diese Rolle vermochte sie nicht zuletzt deshalb zu spielen, da sich der Denar gegen die nach attischer Währung geprägte griechische Drachme austauschen ließ. Die Geldwirtschaft begann sich in dieser Periode auch in Rom als dominierende Form durchzusetzen. Die wirtschaftliche Tätigkeit, die Ausgaben für das tägliche Leben oder die politische Laufbahn erfolgten auf der Grundlage der Münzgeldwirtschaft.

In Rom gab es nach der Mitte des 2. Jh. v. u. Z. das strenge Festhalten an vorgegebenen Münzbildern auf. Die Münzmeister entschieden anscheinend allein darüber, welches Münzbild gewählt wurde. Religiöse, mythologische und historische Themen, auf den römischen Staat, vor allem aber auf die Vorfahren und das Geschlecht der jeweilig amtierenden Münzmeister bezogen, bestimmten in der Folgezeit Art und Inhalt der Darstellungen [7]. Innerhalb weniger Jahrzehnte wurde die römische Münze so zu einem „Tummelplatz der Eitelkeit der großen Geschlechter" (K. Regling) [8], und, was für uns heute wichtiger ist, für die moderne Forschung zu einer Geschichtsquelle von außerordentlich hoher Ergiebigkeit. In dieser Periode beginnt der „Informationsstrom" der Jenaer Sammlung aufgrund stetig sich verdichtender Bestückung breiter zu fließen, läßt sich detaillierter die weitere Geschichte des römischen Geldes verfolgen.

Zunächst erfolgte die Veränderung des stereotypen Münzbildes durch Zufügung von Beizeichen sowie der Namen der Münzmeister. Der Denar des Antestius (Abb. 10) zeigt auf der Vorderseite das traditionelle Münzbild: den behelmten Romakopf und das Wertzeichen X. Hinzugekommen ist als Beizeichen ein laufender Hund hinter dem Romakopf — das Geschlechtersymbol der Antistier. Die Rückseite zeigt neben den traditionellen Darstellungsteilen — die Dioskuren zu Pferde mit eingelegter Lanze sowie die Legende *Roma* im Abschnitt — als neues Element den Namen des Münzmeisters in einer Kurzform: *C. ANTEST.*

Die erste „Geschichtsmünze" im besten Sinne des Wortes bietet der Münzmeister Gaius Minucius Augurinus. Sein Denar (Abb. 11) zeigt auf der Vorderseite zum einen die bereits bekannten Bildteile — behelmter Romakopf, Wertzeichen-, zum anderen die Legende *Roma* als folgenreiche Neuerung. Dadurch, daß Augurinus die Umschrift *Roma* auf die Vorderseite zog, erhielt er mehr Raum für die Rückseitendarstellung. Dieser Münzmeister war der erste, der ihn auch konsequent zur Verherrlichung seines Geschlechtes zu nutzen, mit einfachen Mitteln meisterhaft auszu-

---

[7] M. Crawford, *Geld und Austausch in der römischen Welt,* in: *Sozial- und Wirtschaftsgeschichte der römischen Kaiserzeit,* hrsg. von H. Schneider. Darmstadt 1981, 258—279.

[8] Dieser stufenweise Prozeß wurde zuerst von K. Regling, *Die antike Münze als Kunstwerk.* Berlin 1924, 112 f. charakterisiert.

drücken vermochte, was seine Vorfahren an historischen Verdiensten vorzuzeigen hatten: Das Münzbild zeigt ein Bronzedenkmal, das zur Würdigung der Leistungen seines Vorfahren Lucius Minucius Augurinus 439 v. u. Z. errichtet worden war, weil dieser während einer Hungersnot eine umfassende Getreideversorgung organisiert hatte. Rechts neben dem Monument ist Marcus Minucius Faesus dargestellt, einer der ersten gewählten Auguren, links der Vater des Münzmeisters, der 187 v. u. Z. Volkstribun war.

Die Wiedergabe der *facta maiorum* wurde für mehr als ein halbes Jahrhundert zum beherrschenden Thema der Münzbilder. Im 1. Jh. v. u. Z. begann sich dabei die Verherrlichung der Taten der Vergangenheit immer mehr der Gegenwart zu nähern. Der erste Münzmeister, der 62 v. u. Z. Ereignisse der Zeitgeschichte darstellen ließ, war Faustus Cornelius Sulla, der Sohn des Diktators. Sein Denar zeigt auf der Vorderseite ein „zeitgemäßes" Bild: die Büste der Diana, dazu ein Lituus sowie die Legende *FAUSTUS*. Bedeutsam ist die Rückseitendarstellung, die das Ende des Jugurthinischen Krieges wiedergibt: Sie zeigt Sulla in der Toga auf einem erhöhten Sitz. Auf ihn, als durch Gesetz ernannten Diktator, bezieht sich auch die Legende *FELIX*. Vor ihm kniet, mit einem Friedenszweig (Ölbaum) in den Händen als Zeichen der Unterwerfung, Bocchus, der König von Mauretanien; hinter ihm, gleichfalls kniend, aber mit gefesselten Händen, wird der im Krieg unterlegene Jugurtha gezeigt, der König von Numidien.

Eigene Aktionen (Abb. 12) ließ als erster Marcus Aemilius Scaurus auf Münzen darstellen. Der Stiefsohn des Sulla hatte 58 v. u. Z. gemeinsam mit Publius Plautius Hypsaeus das Münzmeisteramt inne. Während letzterer auf der Rückseite die Tat eines Ahnherrn aus dem Jahre 341 v. u. Z., die Eroberung von Privernum in Erinnerung rief, brachte Scaurus die Unterwerfung des Nabatäerkönigs Aretas auf die Vorderseite: Aretas kniet neben seinem gesattelten Kamel, den Frieden erbittenden Olivenzweig als Zeichen der Unterwerfung haltend. Sehr umfangreich und aussagereich ist auch die Legende: *M. SCAVR.* (= Marcus Scaurus) *AED. CUR.* (= seine staatliche Funktion — *aedilis curulis*), in der Mitte dann *EX. SC* (= der Hinweis auf den besonderen Anlaß — auf Beschluß des Senates geprägt) und im Abschnitt schließlich *REX ARETAS*.

Die Darstellung von Gegenwartsthemen auf den Münzen umfaßte rasch die ganze Breite des gesellschaftlichen und politischen Lebens (Abb. 13)[9]. Es war daher nur eine Frage der Zeit, wann der in der griechisch-hellenistischen Zeit geübte Brauch, das Bildnis des regierenden Monarchen (oder Despoten) auf die Münzvorderseite zu setzen, auch in der römischen Münzprägung Eingang finden würde. Caesar war derjenige,

[9] L. Morawiecki, *Political propaganda in the coinage of the late Roman Republic.* Wrocław u. a. 1983.

der diesen Schritt vollzog. Er tat dies mit besonderer Genehmigung des Senates. Sein Münzmeister Publius Sepullius Macer brachte dieses Caesarbildnis (Abb. 14), — unverwechselbar ausgewiesen durch die Legende *CAESAR DICT. PERPETUO* (Caesar, Diktator auf Lebenszeit) —, während seiner Amtszeit 44 v. u. Z., als mit der Toga bedeckten und bekränzten Kopf. Die Rückseitendarstellung zeigt die Venus Genetrix (mit Victoria, Szepter und Schild) sowie die Signatur des Münzmeisters *P. SEPULLIUS MACER*. Sie hebt so einerseits in ganz traditioneller Weise die kultisch-religiösen Bindungen des Geschlechts des Diktators hervor, wie sie andererseits in republikanischer Tradition verharrend, dem Münzmeister Gelegenheit bot, sich namentlich zu präsentieren.

Alle Machthaber, die nach dem Tode Caesars zu Einfluß und zu Münzprägemöglichkeiten gelangten, — einschließlich der Caesarmörder-, übernahmen wie selbstverständlich das Bildnisprivileg als Münzvorderseitendarstellung. Auch bei den Rückseitenbildern hielten sie an der ganzen inhaltlichen Themenbreite fest, mit der politisch-gesellschaftlich-individuelle Beeinflussung der spätrepublikanisch-römischen Gesellschaft sowie die adäquate Selbstdarstellung der Militärs und Politiker üblich geworden war.

Bild und Stil der römischen Kaisermünzen entwickelten sich zwar ohne Bruch aus dem der republikanischen Prägungen, doch erfuhr das römische Münzwesen unter der Alleinherrschaft des Augustus wesentliche Änderungen. Zunächst machte der Prinzeps die Goldprägung zum festen Bestandteil des römischen Währungssystems und den Aureus zum vorherrschenden Goldnominal. Für drei Jahrhunderte wurde seine Fixierung der wertmäßig präzis abgestuften Dreimetallprägung — Gold, Silber, Aes — bestimmend.

Fast alle Münzwerte tragen von nun an auf der Vorderseite Kopf, Namen und Titel des Kaisers, wobei letztere mehr oder weniger abgekürzt [10] — und, falls bei Interesse des Prägeherren der Raum der Vorderseite nicht ausreichte, auf der Rückseite fortgeführt — erscheinen. Diese Aufführung von Titeln und Ämtern ist es nicht zuletzt, die der modernen Forschung die chronologische Ordnung der kaiserzeitlichen Münzen wesentlich erleichtert, und bisweilen „Feindatierungen" auf Monate genau ermöglicht.

Blieb die Münzvorderseite in der Folgezeit in der Regel dem Porträt des Kaisers — als Symbol der Autorität und der Macht des Staates [11] —

---

[10] Die Legende erscheint in der Folgezeit vor allem in der Abkürzung: *IMP CAES* (Kaisername) *PM TRP* (Zahl) *COS* (Zahl) *PP*. Die mehr oder weniger starken Abkürzungen stehen für: *IMP (erator)*, *CAES(ar)*, *AUG(ustus)*, *P(ontifex) M(aximus)*, *TR(ibunitia) P(otestate)*, *CO(n)S(ul)*, *P(ater) P(atriae)*. Gleiches gibt es auch für Ehren- und Siegesbeinamen — *GERM(anicus)*, *DAC(icus)*, die nicht wenige Kaiser führten.

[11] Andrew Wallace-Hadrill, *Image and authority in the coinage of Augustus*, The journal of Roman studies, 76, 1986, 66—87.

sowie denen seines engsten Familienkreises vorbehalten, so hielt man die Rückseitendarstellungen in ihrer thematischen Weite stets offen, so daß sie sowohl religiöse, mythologische, allegorische oder kunsthistorisch-kulturelle als auch — und dies vor allem — propagandistische Themen (Regierungsprogramme, militärische Erfolge, besondere Leistungen des Kaisers oder Angehöriger des Herrscherhauses u. a.) verbreiten konnten. Da das Münzgeld in allen Reichsteilen zirkulierte, kam den Münzen als Informationsträgern eine stetig wachsende Bedeutung zu.

Ein historisch bedeutsames Detail soll daher am Schluß unserer Betrachtungen stehen — die Reflexion der Thronnachfolge [12] in der augusteischen Münzkunst.

Bereits in der Zeit der Republik war es üblich geworden, beim Fehlen erblicher Söhne zur Sicherung des Fortbestandes der Familien, besonders der einflußreichen Adelsfamilien, einen männlichen Nachfolger zu adoptieren. Bei der Suche nach einem würdigen Erben hielt man zunächst im Kreise der Verwandten Ausschau. In Anwendung dieses Brauches wurde auch Augustus von Caesar, seinem Onkel, adoptiert. Da die Ehe des Princeps mit Livia kinderlos blieb, gestaltete sich für ihn die Nachfolgeregelung äußerst schwierig. Seine Überlegungen und Aktivitäten wurden zunächst mit Julia verbunden, seiner Tochter aus erster Ehe mit Scribonia. Er verheiratete sie 25. v. u. Z. mit seinem Neffen Marcellus. Ehe sich diese Vorstellungen verfestigen konnten, waren sie bereits überlebt, denn Marcellus starb bereits zwei Jahre nach der Eheschließung an einer in Rom ausgebrochenen Seuche.

21 v. u. Z. arrangierte Augustus daher eine Ehe zwischen der nun 18jährigen Julia und dem 41jährigen Agrippa, seinem politischen und militärischen Mitstreiter. Aus dieser Verbindung gingen zwei Söhne und eine Tochter hervor: Gaius und Lucius (geboren 20 bzw. 17 v. u. Z.) und Agrippina (geboren 14 v. u. Z.). Nach der Geburt des Lucius wurden beide Söhne von Augustus adoptiert. Im Jahre 13 v. u. Z. wurden ihre Bildnisse zusammen mit dem ihrer Mutter in der Mitte auf Denaren und Aurei (Abb. 15) [13] abgebildet. Mit dem Tode des Agrippa 12 v. u. Z. rückten sie als Thronprätendenten weiter in den Vordergrund, ihre Propagierung auf den Münzen als präsumptive Nachfolger verstärkte sich.

Zunächst erschien 8 v. u. Z. Gaius Caesar allein auf den Rückseitendarstellungen von Denaren und Aurei (Abb. 16) [14]: Gaius nach rechts galoppierend, hält in der rechten Hand das Schwert, in der linken den Schild. Hinter ihm steht ein Feldzeichen (aquila) zwischen zwei Standarten (Legende: *C. CAES. AUGUS. F*).

---

[12] Differenzierter dargestellt anhand der Jenaer Münzsammlung bei U. Türich, *Die Familienangehörigen des Kaisers Augustus auf den römischen Reichsmünzen.* Diplomarbeit. Jena 1984, 9 ff.

[13] BMC I Augustus Nr. 106, 108 f.

[14] BMC I Augustus 498 ff.; Jena, Sammlung Schmidt Nr. 564.

Das Münzbild bezog sich vermutlich auf die Feierlichkeiten anläßlich der Einführung des Gaius in den Militärdienst [15]. Noch entschiedener erfolgte die Vorstellung der Thronprätendenten auf den in großer Zahl und über Jahre hinweg — 2 v. u. Z. bis spätestens 4 u. Z. — von Augustus herausgegebenen Prägungen, die auf ihren Rückseiten Gaius und Lucius Caesares als *principes iuventutis* vorstellen (Abb. 17).

Gaius und Lucius, bekleidet mit der Toga, halten jeweils Schild und Speer; zwischen den Speeren befinden sich im oberen Bildteil die Priestersymbole lituus und simplum. Die Legende lautet: *C L CAESARES AUGUSTI F COS DESIG PRINC IVVENT*.

Die Darstellung bezieht sich eigentlich auf ein „Alltagsgeschehen" — die feierliche Volljährigkeitserklärung. Sie war immer mit der Eintragung in das Bürgerverzeichnis verknüpft, die wiederum eine Voraussetzung für die Berechtigung zur Wahrnehmung der bürgerlichen Rechte bildete. Augustus gab in diesem Falle durch die öffentliche Vorstellung seiner beiden Adoptivsöhne im Rahmen ihrer Volljährigkeitserklärung auf dem Forum Romanum 2 v. u. Z. den Rang eines staatspolitisch wichtigen Ereignisses [16]. Er verband diesen Vorgang zudem mit der Einführung von Gaius und Lucius Caesares in die Staatsangelegenheiten, indem er sie nicht nur erstmals an den öffentlichen Senatssitzungen teilnehmen, sondern auf breiterer Grundlage auch ihre herausragende gesellschaftlich-politische Position bestätigen ließ: Durch den Senat wurden sie zu Consuln designiert, und die römische Ritterschaft verlieh ihnen den Titel principes iuventutis. Aus Anlaß dieser Ehrung überreichte man ihnen jeweils — in Form silberner Zeremoniellwaffen — einen Rundschild und einen Speer. Die im Münzbild hinzugefügten Symbole lituus und simplum wiesen ihr Wirken in höchsten Priesterämtern aus, als pontifex (*simplum* — Gaius) und augur (*lituus* — Lucius).

Der Titel princeps iuventutis zeichnet die beiden Thronprätendenten als Führer der Ritterschaft aus. Sie waren die ersten präsumptiven Nachfolger, die ihn trugen. Von nun an wurde die Verleihung dieses Titels an vorgesehene Thronnachfolger zur Regel.

Die Hoffnungen, die Augustus auf die Söhne des Agrippa und der Julia als Erben setzte, erfüllten sich nicht: Lucius starb 2 v. u. Z. in Massilia, Gaius 4 u. Z. an einer Verwundung, die er im Krieg gegen die Parther erhalten hatte. Für den Princeps war die Nachfolgefrage so wieder ungelöst.

---

[15] Die Interpretation des Münzbildes ist in der wissenschaftlichen Literatur nicht einheitlich. Andere Deutungsmöglichkeiten sind z. B.: Teilnahme des 12-jährigen Gaius am Germanenfeldzug des Tiberius oder Vorstellung des jungen Thronprätendenten bei den rheinischen Legionen. Vgl. D. Kienast, *Augustus-Princeps und Monarch.* Darmstadt 1982, bes. S. 106 und 323.

[16] Th. Fischer, *Zur Münzprägung des Augustus für seine beiden Adoptivsöhne Gaius und Lucius Caesar,* in: Lagom. Festschrift für Peter Berghaus. Münster 1981, bes. 35 f.

Für ihn scheint es kein leichter Entschluß gewesen zusein, Tiberius Claudius Nero, den Sohn der Livia, zu adoptieren und zu seinem Nachfolger [17] zu bestimmen, der unter dem Namen Kaiser Tiberius bekannt geworden ist. Dieser erscheint erstmals 9 u. Z. auf Reichsprägungen, doch soll hier der stufenweise sich vollziehende Prozeß seiner Popularisierung als Thronprätendent nicht nachvollzogen werden.

Schließen wir ab. Die Münzen als die am vollständigsten erhaltene, alle Perioden gleichmäßig erfassende Denkmälergruppe sind heute zu einer der wichtigsten Quellen für Studien zur politischen, zur Kunst-, Religions- und Wirtschaftsgeschichte geworden. Die Jenenser Münzsammlungen bieten eine solide Ausgangsbasis für weiterführende Studien. Diesbezüglich bislang kaum erschlossen, liegt hier noch ein weites Arbeitsfeld für die nachdrängende Wissenschaftlergeneration.

Titelbild. (vor dem Aufsatz stehend) Aureus des Nero mit der Darstellung des geschlossenen Janustempels (Sammlung Schmidt Nr. 787)

---

[17] H. U. Instinsky, *Augustus und die Adoption des Tiberius,* Hermes 94, 1966, 324—343.

Andrzej Laska
Kraków

GLASS REPRODUCTIONS OF ANCIENT GEMS IN THE COLLECTIONS OF THE JAGELLONIAN UNIVERSITY MUSEUM

Starting from the ancient times and continuedly up till the latter half of the 18th century, gems as well as their glass reproductions used to serve solely utilitarian and aesthetic purposes. They were assigned practical value as seals, ornaments, amulets, appliqués and the like. The launching of archaeological investigations at Pompeii and Herculaneum as well as the studies by J. Winckelmann called anew the attention of critics and collectors to the art of antiquity, including also the miniature products of that epoch, i. e. intaglios and cameos.

Consequently, it was thenceforth that a new significance came to be attached to gem collections (the *dactyliothecae*). Assembled in growing numbers and in conditions of accomodation specifically designed for the purpose, they became, along with coins, vases, reliefs, oil lamps and the like, a relevant source of iconography for the nascent systematic research on ancient art and culture [1].

The above-mentioned characteristic and, likewise, a hampered access to many private collections contributed to the necessity of making cast reproductions from original gems. Multiple sets were therefore formed, which, among other uses, were turned to didactic and research purposes. By the same token, the methodology of instruction was enhanced and diversified. The materials used to produce the casts included sulphur, gypsum, clay, glass (called paste or strass), lead, and even sealing-wax.

Against a background thus delineated, it is to the credit of the reformed Cracow Academy that, following as early as the 80s of the 18th century, the University enjoyed and employed such aids. As evidence of this,

---

[1] The most recent studies on ancient gliptic see P. Z a z o f f, *Die Antiken Gemmen*, München 1983 and the same author *Gemmensammler und Gemmenforscher*. München 1983.

the University Library of that time held a collection of 1005 sulphur casts with designs in ancient motifs as well as a collection of 37 paste gems acquired some time after [2].

Although Emanuel Murray (a Frenchman settled in Poland), while writing a guidebook of Kraków, made a note in *Opisanie Biblioteki Akademickiej* in 1787 that there were "Impresses [...] in sealing-wax or some similar composition ..." [3] there as well, a source apparently meriting more credibility is the entry recorded in *Inwentarz Biblioteki Jagiellońskiej* (an 1840 inventory of the Jagiellonian Library), according to which those were "... casts from ancient cameos with red sulphur as the material ..." [4]

The above-mentioned Inventory of 1840, p. 133 (Nos. 1—3), contains information testifying to the possession by the Library of three ancient (?) cameos with representations of M. Cicero, his son and Pyrrhus, king of Epirus. It was, nevertheless, as early as May 1864 that all the three cameos were consigned to disposal by the Scientific Society of Cracow (Towarzystwo Naukowe Krakowskie), the predecessor to the later Academy of Arts and Letters (Akademia Umiejętności) [5].

---

[2] A catalogue of this collection entitled *Dactyliotheca*, recorded in French, has been preserved at the Jagellonian Library (Manuscripts Section, No. 1049). A list of the afore-mentioned 37 paste pieces was appended to the end of the catalogue a dozen or so years later, already following the note made by F. Oraczewski in 1786.

Sulphur casts included among their representations images of gods, philosophers, heroes of Troy, Roman consuls and emperors. However, considering the form of descriptive characterizations concerning each piece (entries specifying theme, variety of the original gem and, very rarely, a cameo's contemporary owner and the engraver's name), the dates of the making of the originals are not amenable to a precise determination. The paste reproductions, on the other hand, were made from gems produced by modern glyptic engravers, such as L. Pichler (1773—1854) or G. Girometti (1779—1851), those drawing, in turn, on works by A. Canova and B. Thorvaldsen.

[3] E. Murray, *Opisanie topograficzne i filozoficzne miasta Krakowa* (comp. K. Estreicher Jr.), Rocznik Krakowski, XLVIII, 1977, p. 148.

[4] The inventory is kept at the Jagiellonian Library, the Manuscripts Section, and bears no cataloguing specifications. The data cited appears on pages 126—127. On page 127 a reference can be found to the 37 pastes recorded in *Dactyliotheca* as well as mention is made identifying as Pietro Bracci the maker behind them, with Rome the place of origin.

[5] *Wykaz przedmiotów wskutek reskryptu Wysokiego c.k. Ministerstwa Stanu z dn. 11 Października 1863 r. Licz. 8725 z Biblioteki Uniwersytetu Jagiellońskiego przez Towarzystwo Naukowe Krakowskie odebranych (List of properties seized from the Jagellonian University Library by the Scientific Society of Cracow consequent upon of the High Imperial and Royal Ministry of State, as of October 11th, No. 8725)*, [in:] Zbiory archeologiczne. Archeologia. Numizmata. Obrazy z lat 1840—1866, entries 129, 130, 131. The record comprises a collection of loose letters, manuscripts etc., kept in the Manuscripts Section of the Jagellonian Library. No cataloguing specifications are included in it in its own right, either. The committal previously referred to is certified by date and signature, May 23rd, 1864, H. Seredyński, *Treasurer to the Scientific Society of Cracow*. Also 37 pastes were transferred to this Society.

Fig. 1. Silenus   Fig. 2. Serapis

Fig. 3. Helios in a quadriga

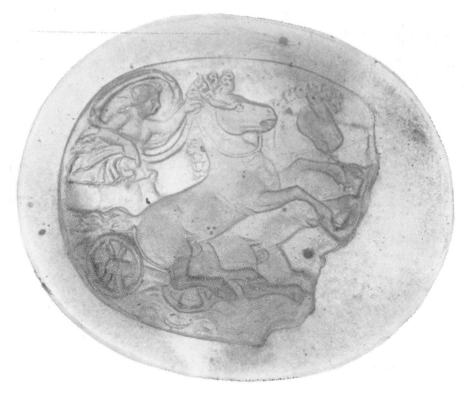

Fig. 4. Selene riding a two-horse chariot

Fig. 5. Nereid astride a hippocampus

About the year 1872 the Archaeological Cabinet of the Jagellonian University received a donation from Władysław Czartoryski, consisting of 445 gypsum casts from intaglios and cameos [6]. Several years afterwards, between 1875 and 1880, the Archaeological Cabinet acquired additional 32 glass casts from coins, medals and cameos. Ornamented with representations of antique motifs, they had been made and offered by L. W. Pantoczek (1812—1893) [7]. No further bequests of like character are on record following that.

Currently, the collections of the Jagellonian University Museum, Art Craft Section, feature 47 gypsum as well as 9 glass casts from gems [8]. Among the 47 gypsum casts, which most probably are the remainder of W. Czartoryski's donation, 24 pieces bear depictions of antique themes (portraits of emperors and philosophers), whereas the remaining ones are adorned with images of contemporary figures [9]. All of the 47 reproductions

---

[6] *Inwentarz Gabinetu Archeologicznego UJ (Inventory of the Archaeological Cabinet of the Jagellonian University)*, entry 6685. Kept at the Jagellonian University Museum. Subsequent notes specify: "ilość 445" (quantity of 445). No data is available, however, concerning the material of which they were made and the representational thematic scope covered thereon.

[7] *Ibidem*, entry 7040. The casts themselves are lost. Only a small case in which they were kept has been preserved. A label affixed to it indicates that the reproductions were cast in the J. Zahn glass factory at Zlatno (Slovakia). Compare also: M. Tyrowicz, *Pantoczek Leon Walenty* (1812—1893), [in:] *PSB*, XXV, 1980, p. 150. L. W. Pantoczek, a physician by education and a chemist by election, originated new methods in the field of glass technology, including, for instance, employment of opal in glazing (hyaloplastics) or modifications and refinements in the manufacture of crystal glass.

[8] Moreover: an onyx cameo with an image of Primate Michał Poniatowski made by G. Santarelli (1758—1826) as well as two glass casts of cameos with portraits of Antoni Radziwiłł and Tadeusz Kościuszko, which are reproductions of works by J. Regulski (1760—1807). Cf. A. Laska, *Kolekcjonerzy i grawerzy gemm w Polsce w XVI—XIX wieku*, Opuscula Musealia, 1, 1986, pp. 9—31.

[9] An oral account as conveyed to the author of this article by Prof. K. Estreicher Jr. implies that the latter located the above-mentioned 47 gypsum casts in the new building of the Jagellonian Library in Mickiewicz Street, already subsequent to World War II. It was there that the book collection and some of the property had been moved from the Collegium Maius starting from 1940. This evidence appears to reinforce the theory that the gypsum pieces constitute a surviving remainder of W. Czartoryski's donation (445 casts). This is also corroborated by the fact that some of them bear on their paper mounts comparatively high identification numbers, such as "165", "166", the number "311" incised on the reverse side of one of the casts.

As regards the technique of creation, i.e. the type of material, mode of mounting and numbering, the gypsum casts collection displays homogeneity. The only identified image among treated modern figures is the representation of Joseph Buonaparte with a band around his head. Since the headband is a symbol of royal authority, which, as is know, he wielded between 1806 and 1808 at Naples and in the years 1808—1813 in Spain, it follows, at the present stage of research, that the cast in question is susceptible of being construed as pinpointing the earliest time watershed signifying the terminus post quem to which the whole collection can be dated.

had been modelled on works of contemporary glyptic engravers, with antique prototypes to a large extent an inspiring source behind.

As for the glass casts, they constitute a group of eight oval objects with representations executed in high relief, complemented by semirounded representation of Serapis' head [10]. Four of the reproductions were made from 18th and 19th century gems [11]. The remaining five casts, of prime interest here, were made from originals dated to the Hellenistic and Roman period (Cat. Nos. 1—5).

The foregoing evidence thus indicates that the current collection of glass and gypsum gem reproductions at the Jagiellonian University Museum commands no remarkable significance either in terms of quantity or relative appeal of the reproduced models. It is, nonetheless, a manifestation of the considerable attraction towards objects of this kind exhibited by scholars and collectors especially in the 18th and 19th centuries.

CATALOGUE

Abbreviations

EAA — *Enciclopedia dell'Arte Antica Classica e Orientale.*
Furtwängler — A. Furtwängler, *Die Antiken Gemmen*, I—III. Berlin—Leipzig 1900.
J. U. — Jagellonian University.
PSB — *Polski Słownik Biograficzny.*
Roscher — W. H. Roscher, *Ausführliches Lexikon der Griechischen und Römischen Mythologie.*
Walters, *Gems* — H. B. Walters, *Catalogue of the Engraved Gems and Cameos Greek, Etruscan and Roman in the British Museum.* London 1926.
Walters, *Lamps* — H. B. Walters, *Catalogue of the Greek and Roman Lamps in the British Museum.* London 1914.

---

[10] The information on the provenience of the glass casts, too, proceeds from Prof. K. Estreicher Jr., and was imparted to the author indirectly by the former Deputy Director of the Jagellonian University Museum, Dr. K. Nowacki. This evidence indicates that the casts were reclaimed after World War II by K. Estreicher, Silesia being probably the venue involved in the restitution.

[11] These comprise: a representation of the head of Menelaus, white, opaque glass [the original from which the impression concerned was derived had been made by N. Marchant (1739—1816), J. U. Museum Inv. No. 7302]; a representation of the head of Serapis (with a modius), two-layered glass, milky-transparent, J. U. Museum Inv. No. 7303; a representation of the head of Athena (with the Corinthian helmet on), after the original by L. Pichler, two-layered glass, milky-transparent, J. U. Museum inv. no. 8723; the bust of a bacchante (or Pomona?), dark blue glass, J. U. Museum Inv. No. 7305.

1. Silenus' head (Fig. 1)

Two-layered glass, milky in colour on the relief side, with transparent background.
Dim.: 22 × 26 × 5 mm.
Inv. No.: 8720.

Head en face of a bearded old man, in an oval sunken field. Ivy wreath surmounting balding forehead. Broad facial outline, deeply and closely set eyes. Fringe of hair growth on face, short and desultorily delineated. Animal features, such as goat's or pointed ears, lacking, whence, coupled with stylistic analogies, the disputable dating of the original for reproduction in question, either to the Hellenistic or the Roman period.

Cf.: E. Kuhnert, *Satyros und Silenos*, [in:] Roscher, IV, 1909—15, cols. 444—531; P. E. Arias, *Satiri e Sileni*, [in:] *EAA*, VII, 1966, pp. 67—73; Walters, *Gems*, No. 1569, Fig. XXI; Walters, *Lamps*, No. 58, Fig. XI, No. 403, Fig. XIII (lamps from the Hellenistic and Roman period).

2. Serapis (Fig. 2)

White glass.
Dim.: 33 × 22 × 8 mm.
Inv. No.: 7301.

Head of the god in a semirounded sculpture featuring *calathus* adorned with olive leaves. Back of the head worked flat. Face fringed with thick hair. Hairs of the head, falling over the forehead in five curling wisps, steam down the cheeks in long ringlets and merge with the thick, closely twining beard parted along midline. All elaborated very conscientiously with evident meticulousness over detail, marked by fine workmanship of engraving as well as a firm grasp of the subject.

An identical treatment of the head of the god in question, in respect of both facial anatomy and format, is to be found in a cameo dated to the Hellenistic or the Roman period and kept in the Farnese collections in Naples. A. Furtwängler reproduces only an impression made from this cameo, which is distinguishable from the piece under consideration (the one in the keeping of the Jagellonian University Museum) in its having a flat, oval background.

Cf.: M. P. Weitz, *Serapis*, [in:] Roscher, IV, 1909—15, cols. 338—382; L. Vlad Borrelli, *Sarapide*, [in:] *EAA*, VII, 1966, pp. 204—207; Furtwängler, I, No. 10, Fig. LIX and II, pp. 266—267, No. 10; G. Lippold, *Gemmen und Kameen des Altertums und der Neuzeit*. Stuttgart 1912, p. 168, No. 1, Fig. IV.

3. Helios in a quadriga (Fig. 3)

Two-layered glass, milky in colour on the relief side, with transparent background.
Dim.: 32 × 36 × 4 mm.
Inv. No.: 8721.

A nude man riding a quadriga, rendered in low-projection haut-relief. Right hand holding a flambeau, the left one, faintly accentuated, a spear. Overhead, a semicircular line marking the hem of a cloak spread in the sweep of movement. Beneath the quadriga, reclining figure of a man leaning, torso bared and legs draped in cloth, with left, elbow-bent arm in support. Aloft his head, proximate to the rim of impress, a female figure, head inclining toward the recumbent man. The reverse of a Latin inscription, "LAVR MED", above the quadriga. The whole treated with considerable artistic ease and conspicuous effortlessness, the detail of horses afeam imparting a quality of dynamism to the entire scene. Despite the relative by low-profile set of the relief, the total, due to a precise modelling of all the figures, yields substantial distinctness of feature.

An identical representation, as regards all the details, is discernible in a piece on file in the Berlin collections, which is a reproduction of a cameo preserved in the Farnese collections in Naples.

The scene depicted on the cast in question images Helios riding the quadriga, the lying male figure identifiable as Oceanus, the female one probably a Nereid (Thetis?). The inscription borne on the cameo and reproduced on the casts is a later, 15th century addition, an abbreviation of the name of the owner at that time, Lorenzo Medici (1449—1492).

Cf.: A. Rapp, *Helios*, [in:] Roscher, I, 1884—90, cols. 1993—2026; H. Sichtermann, *Helios*, [in:] *EAA*, III, 1960, pp. 1140—1142; Furtwängler, I, No. 27, Fig. XLII; ibidem, II, p. 201, No. 27, cameo from the Farnese collections, made of carnelian, dated to the Hellenistic or the Roman period.

4. Selene riding a two-horse chariot (Fig. 4)

Frosted glass, translucid.
Dim.: 47 × 40 × 6 mm.
Inv. No.: 8722.

The relief section pronouncedly differentiated from the background, delimited, slantways, the side featuring heads and forelegs of the two horses, by an irregular line indicating the contour of a fractured part in the original.

The scene portrays an erect female figure riding a chariot with a two-horse team in harness. The woman's head is adorned with a wreath, torso half-stripped. Left hand of the rider in contact with the horse's mane, foreground, the right hand holding reins. Above the figure, a cloak swung into disarray in rush of progress. The relief executed in suave, harmonious contours.

A representation of a like type (but the whole turned left) is to be found on a cameo from the Hellenistic and Roman period, kept in the British Museum collections. However, the elaboration of the figure on the cameo proves uninspired and unimaginative as compared to that on the cast in the Jagellonian University Museum collections.

Cf.: W. M. Roscher, *Selene,* [in:] Roscher, IV, 1909—15, cols. 642—650; E. Paribeni, *Selene,* [in:] *EAA*, VII, 1966, pp. 168—170; Walters, *Gems*, No. 3528, Fig. XXXVII, cameo made of sardonyx; C. Robert, *Die Antiken Sarkophag-Reliefs*, III₁, 1897, pp. 84—85, No. 71₁, Fig. XVIIa, sarcophagus from the Roman period.

5. Nereid astride a hippocampus (Fig. 5)

Celadon-colour glass.
Dim.: 31 × 39 × 4 mm.
Inv. No.: 7304.

A representation of a half-nude woman mounted on one of two hippocampi in an oval, depressed field. Left hand resting against the monster's tail, the right one holding reins. One foot lapped over the other. A mantle flowing loose apparent to the back, behind the female figure. A dolphin is represented in the field bounded by the legs of the hippocampus and those of the Nereid. The figure of a cupid in view, middle ground, above the legs of the hippocampus. Over the heads of the sea monsters, in high relief, a Latin inscription, "LAVR M" / E D, an abbreviated rendering of the name of the cameo's 15th century owner — Lorenzo Medici.

An identical representation with regard to all the details can be found in a cameo at the Florence museum. A. Furtwängler dates the item to the Hellenistic period. The only dissimilarity between the pieces under consideration consists in the original carrying no framing.

Cf.: P. Weizsäcker, *Nereiden,* [in:] Roscher, III, 1897—1902, cols. 207—240; H. Sichtermann, *Nereo e Nereidi,* [in:] *EAA*, V, 1963, pp. 421—423; Furtwängler, I, No. 43, Fig. XLI and: II, p. 198, No. 43, cast from the Florence cameo; G. Lippold, *Gemmen* ..., p. 168, No. 2, Fig. VII. The author dates the making of the original to the Roman period.

Janusz A. Ostrowski
Kraków

JAN MATEJKO UND DAS ARCHÄOLOGISCHE KABINETT DER JAGIELLONEN-UNIVERSITÄT

Es gibt Denkmäler, die zwar keinen besonders hohen künstlerischen Rang beanspruchen oder einen bemerkenswerten Erkenntnisgewinn vermitteln können, die aber trotzalldem wegen ihres „emotionellen Wertes" ausgesprochen wertvoll sind. Das gilt vor allem für Gegenstände, die mit herausragenden Persönlichkeiten in der Geschichte eines Volkes in Verbindung gebracht werden können, verdienstvollen Staatsmännern, Literaten, Künstlern oder Gelehrten. Diese Materialien, die entweder zielgerichtet von den Museen gesammelt oder erworben, bisweilen von ihren einstigen Besitzern in ihren Häusern zurückgelassen wurden, bilden, zusammen mit der Atmosphäre des Hauses, seiner Ausstattung usw., jenen Teil des Hintergrundes, vor dem die schöpferische Persönlichkeit schärfere Konturen anzunehmen beginnt [1]. Über einen solchen „emotionellen Wert" verfügen auch diejenigen Objekte, die von künstlerischen und historischen Persönlichkeiten zwar nicht benutzt, wohl aber von ihnen erworben

---

[1] Häuser berühmter Künstler erfreuen sich besonderer Fürsorge, und dies gewöhnlich von dem Zeitpunkt an, wo dies bekannt wird. Beispielsweise seien genannt: Rafaels Haus in Urbino, El Grecos Haus in Toledo, Rembrandts Haus in Amsterdam, Frans Halsens Haus in Harlem, Rubens Haus in Antwerpen, Delacroix' Haus in Paris. Ähnlich war es bei Dichterhäusern: denen von J. W. Goethe und F. Schiller (auch dem von F. Liszt) in Weimar, dem Haus Shakespeares in Stratford on Avon, oder in Polen: die Häuser von Żeromski und Prus in Nałęczów und viele andere.

Ein anderes Problem ist die Gründung eines biographischen Museums des Künstlers, das seine Einrichtung entweder der Willensentscheidung des Künstlers selbst (z. B. das Musée Rodin in Paris) verdankt, aus der Stiftung eines Sammlers oder Mäzens resultiert oder als Staats- oder Stadtstiftung entsteht; Ziel der Gründung ist es, hervorragende Bürger zu ehren. Zu der letzteren Gruppe gehört das Jan-Matejko-Haus in Kraków (z. Z. Abteilung des Nationalmuseums).

worden sind. Den diesbezüglichen Aktivitäten der Museen kommt bei der Entwicklung des Geistes- und Wissenschaftslebens eine große Bedeutung zu.

Zu den Denkmälern der charakteriesierten Art gehören drei kleine Tongefäße aus dem 2. Jh. u. Z. (Abb. 1—3) und zwei römische Tonlampen aus dem 1. und 3. Jh. u. Z. (Abb. 4—5) [2]. Sie werden in den Sammlungen des Lehrstuhle für Mittelmeerarchäologie der Jagiellonen-Universität aufbewahrt und sind eine Schenkung, die der bedeutende polnische Maler Jan Matejko (24. VI. 1838 — 1. XI. 1893) dem Archäologischen Kabinett der Krakauer Universität machte. Letzteres bestand vom Jahre 1864 an, erhielt seine festen organisatorischen Formen erst seit 1871 [3]. Der im Exil in Paris weilende Fürst Władysław Czartoryski [4] hatte der Universität eine reiche, über 200 Objekte zählende Schenkung an antiken Gegenständen (griechische Vasen, Terrakotten, Bronzen, Lampen) gemacht. Im gleichen Jahr unternahm Jan Matejko eine seiner zahlreichen Auslandsreisen. Abgesehen von seinen kurzen Studienreisen nach München und Wien [5],

---

[2] Es sind: 1) Amphoriskos (Abb. 1) mit zwei in der breitesten Bauchpartie horizontal aufgesetzten Henkeln, einem ziemlich hohen, rapid in einen flachen Ausguss übergehenden Hals. Gelb-roter Ton, Spuren eines schwarz-braunen Firnisses. Höhe 0,115 m, Durchmesser 0,07 m. Inventarnummer 10.143. Aus Ephesus (?). Bibliographie: *CVA* Pologne 2, Taf. 1 (74), 4; *Zabytki archeologiczne Zakładu Archeologii Śródziemnomorskiej UJ. Katalog.* Kollektivarbeit, hrsg. von M. L. Bernhard. Kraków 1976 (im weiteren als Katalog zitiert), Nr. 468; 2) Flakon (Abb. 2), das in seiner Form den Glasphiolen aus dem 2. Jh. u. Z. ähnlich ist. Hellrosafarbiger Ton. Braune Oberschicht. Höhe 0,116 m, Durchmesser 0,038 m. Inventarnummer 10.144. Aus Brussa. Bibliographie: *CVA* Pologne 2, Taf. 1 (74), 5; *Katalog*, Nr. 469; 3) Flakon (Abb. 3) mit einem unten engen, aufwärts breiter werdenden und beim Hals sich wiederum verjüngenden Bauch. Hellgelber Ton. Schwarzbrauner Firnis. Höhe 0,098 m, Durchmesser 0,043 m. Inventarnummer 10.314. Aus Brussa. Bibliographie: *CVA* Pologne 2, Taf. 1 (74), 6; *Katalog*, Nr. 470; 4) Öllampe (Abb. 4). Gelbgrauer Ton. Lange 0,082 m, Breite 0,055 m. Inventarnummer 10.395. Bibliographie: *Katalog*, Nr. 487. 1 Jh. u. Z.; 5) Öllampe (Abb. 5). Rotbrauner Ton. Lange 0,095 m, Breite 0,055 m. Inventarnummer 10.406. Bibliographie: *Katalog*, Nr. 520. 3 Jh. u. Z.

[3] M. L. Bernhard, *Historia zbioru*, [in:] *Katalog*, S. 9—18; J. Śliwa, *Zur Geschichte der Antikensammlung an der Jagiellonen-Universität*, Wissenschaftliche Beiträge der Friedrich-Schiller-Universität. Jena 1985, S. 54—66.

[4] Władysław Czartoryski (1828—1894), der Sohn von Adam Jerzy Czartoryski, wurde nach dem Tode seines Vaters 1881 zum Führer der polnischen Emigranten in Frankreich. Mit Napoleon III verbunden, war er ein Fürsprecher einer französisch-österreichischer Zusammenarbeit gegen Russland und Preussen. Neben seiner politischen Tätigkeit machte er sich auch als Sammler einen Namen, indem er die von seiner Grossmutter Izabela Czartoryska, geb. Flemming und seinem Vater angelegte letzte Sammlung, eine der reichsten polnischen Kunstsammlungen, vergrößerte. 1876 wurde diese Sammlung aus Paris (Hôtel Lambert) nach Kraków verlegt und das Czartoryski-Museum (z. Z. Abteilung des Nationalmuseums in Kraków) gegründet. Vgl. M. Kukiel, in: *Polski Słownik Biograficzny* (= *PSB*), Bd. 4, 1938, S. 300—303.

[5] Matejko studierte zunächst in Kraków, dann von Januar bis Juli 1859 in München, u. a. bei Prof. A. Anschütz. In Wien weilte er lediglich zwei Monate lang und studierte

reiste Matejko vorwiegend nach Paris und Wien, diesmal führte aber seine Route nach Süd-Osten.

Als Ziel der von Jan Matejko zusammen mit seiner Frau Teodora unternommenen Reise galt die Türkei, genauer gesagt Istanbul und Umgebung. Er reiste in ein Land, in welchem nach den Niederlagen der nationalen Aufstände von 1830, 1848 und 1863 viele Polen Obdach gesucht hatten. Insbesondere die beiden zuerstgenannten Aufstände haben zur Vergrößerung der Zahl der in der Türkei lebenden Polen beigetragen. Die polnische Exil-Regierung, die zunächst in London, seit 1833 unter Führung des Fürsten Adam Jerzy Czartoryski in Paris arbeitete [6], hatte die Türkei als ein Land ausgesucht, wo zahlreiche Emissäre die zwischen Russland und der Otomanischen Pforte bestehenden Gegensätze zum Nutzen der Polen auszuspielen versuchten. In der Türkei entstand 1842 ein polnisches Dorf namens Czartoryskis Adampol (z. Z. Polonezköy), in dem sich viele Emigranten niederließen [7]. Von den zahlreichen Polen, die in der Türkei tätig waren, seien einige Namen genannt: besonders beachtenswert ist Michał Czajkowski (1804—1886), der im Exil in den Jahren 1831—1872 lebte [8]. 1850 war er zum Islam übergetreten [9] und

---

bei dem Akademiedirektor Ruben. Ein aus der Kompositionsbeurteilung einer Skizze Matejkos zum Bild *Jan Kazimierz in Bielany nach der Flucht aus Krakau* resultierender Konflikt mit einem der Professoren der Wiener Akademie ließ Matejko diese Einrichtung schon bald wieder verlassen. Der Professor war der Meinung, das Bild sei zwar gut gemalt, nur erfordere es, daß der König knie, worauf Matejko erwiderte, daß „polnische Könige vor niemandem gekniet hätten".

[6] Adam Jerzy Czartoryski (1770—1861) wurde in der Jugend als Loyalitätsgeisel der Familie Czartoryski an den Hof der Zarin Katharina II. geschickt, wo er sich die Freundschaft Alexander I. erwarb. Während dessen Regierung bekleidete er hohe Ämter in der russischen Verwaltung und zwar zugleich Führer der legalen Opposition. Nachdem sich Adam Jerzy Czartoryski dem Novemberaufstand 1831 angeschlossen hatte, wurden die Güter der Familie Czartoryski eingezogen und er selbst in Abwesenheit zum Tode verurteilt. Nach der Niederlage des Aufstands ging er ins Exil. Eine Chance für die Wiederherstellung der Souveränität Polens sah er in der antirussischen Politik der westeuropäischen Länder sowie in der Entwicklung nationaler Befreiungsbewegungen in Südosteuropa. Vgl. M. Handelsman, in: *PSB* 4, 1938, S. 257—269.

[7] Vgl. K. Dopierała, *Adampol — Polonezköy. Z dziejów Polaków w Turcji*. Poznań 1983.

[8] Nach der Niederlage des Novemberaufstandes ging Czajkowski nach Frankreich, dann ab 1841 in die Türkei. Nach 1863 unterlag er den Panslawismus-Ideen und mit dem Wohlwollen des Zaren ließ er sich in der Ukraine nieder. Er war Verfasser zahlreicher, im Geiste romantischer Idealisierung des Kosakentums geschriebener Romane, Bücher, die Leben der Balkanslawen und Geschichte Polens betrachteten. Czajkowski hinterließ auch sehr interessante Tagebücher, 1886 beging er Selbstmord. Zum Czajkowskis Lebenslauf vgl. J. Chudzikowska, *Dziwne życie Sadyka Paszy. O Michale Czajkowskim*. Warszawa 1971 und Jerzy S. Łątka, *Carogrodzki pojedynek*. Kraków 1985.

[9] Der Übertritt zum Islam erfolgte nicht freiwillig. Die türkische Regierung stellte die Alternative: den Mohammedanismus annehmen und in der Türkei in die Dienste des Sultans treten oder — Deportation und Auslieferung an Russland, was dem Tode

wurde im türkischen Dienst als Mehmed Sadyk oder Sadyk Pascha bekannt. Während des Krimkrieges (1853—1856) führte er eine von ihm gebildete Abteilung der Sultankosaken. Zusammen mit ihm arbeitete Antoni Aleksander Ilinski (1814—1861), der ein unstetes und abenteuerliches Leben führte und, nachdem er den Islam 1847 angenommen hatte, als Bej (ab 1856 als Pascha) Iskander wirkte [10]. Nach der Niederlage des ungarischen Aufstandes im Jahre 1849 — in dem der Bruder von Jan Matejko — Zygmunt gefallen war — fanden viele Polen und Ungarn (L. Kossuth) ihr Obdach in der Türkei. Dies führte zu Spannungen in den Beziehungen zwischen dem Zaren und dem Sultan. Der bedeutenste der ehemaligen Teilnehmer des ungarischen Aufstands war General Józef Bem (1794—1850). Er trat dem Islam bei und begann beim Sultan als Murad Pascha zu dienen. Nach Aleppo geschickt, verstarb der General schon bald in dieser syrischen Stadt [11].

Der Krimkrieg hatte in den Polen die Hoffnung geweckt, Russland von der türkischen Seite angreifen und so von Süden her in die Heimat zurückkehren zu können. Der polnische Dichter Adam Mickiewicz kam

---

oder langjähriger Verschickung gleich kam. Es ist bemerkenswert, daß die Türken polnische Offiziere schätzten und ihnen hohe Stellungen in der türkischen Armee anvertrauten.

[10] Von der Tätigkeit Ilinskis wissen wir viel, trotzdem können wir nicht sicher sein, ob alle überlieferten Geschehnisse seines Lebens in Wirklichkeit stattfanden. Ilinski bildete eine Legende um sich selbst. Nach der Niederlage des Novemberaufstands war er in Frankreich, dann kämpfte er in Portugal und Spanien (wo er angeblich in feindliche Hände geriet und beinahe erschossen worden wäre, sich aber durch bravouröse Flucht retten konnte; in Spanien soll er sich angeblich als Stierkämpfer versucht haben). Dann ging er zur Fremdenlegion, die in dieser Zeit in Algerien eingesetzt war. Daraufhin kämpfte er sich bis nach Afghanistan durch, wo er an der Belagerung Herats durch Perser 1836 teilgenommen haben soll. Vielleicht gelangte er nach Indien, sogar auch nach China. Seit 1844 war er in der Türkei, anfänglich unter der griechisch-orthodoxen Balkan-Bevölkerung. Er agitierte dagegen, den Zaren als Haupt der Balkankirchen zu verehren und trat dafür ein, den Konstantinopler Patriarchen an dessen Stelle zu sehen. Ilinski hat es erreicht, daß in vielen Dörfern und Kirchen für den Zaren nicht mehr gebetet wurde. Nachdem er in den Sultandienst getreten war, kämpfte er u. a. während des Krimkrieges und führte bei Eupatoria im Februar 1855 einen ausgezeichneten Kavallerieangriff, wofür ihm der Brigadegeneralsgrad und der Paschatitel verliehen wurden. Ilinski bekam damals vom Sultan einen mit Diamanten besetzten Säbel, welchen er angeblich sofort im Kartenspiel verloren haben soll. Zum Ilinskis Lebenslauf vgl. Chudzikowska, *Dziwne życie* ... und Łątka, *Carogrodzki pojedynek*, passim.

[11] General Bem suchte während seines Aufenthaltes in Syrien nach Möglichkeiten, Araber für einen eventuellen Krieg gegen Rußland zu gewinnen. Zum Bems Lebenslauf vgl. W. Tokarz, in: *PSB* 1, 1935, S. 416—419. Es ist betonenswert, daß 1833 und 1834 Major Ludwik Bystrzonowski in Syrien (auch in Ägypten) weilte, der Stifter des ersten, in polnischen Sammlungen befindlichen ägyptischen Sarkophags aus den Zeiten der XXI—XXII Dynastie, welcher der Jagiellonen-Universität am 17. Mai 1834 übergeben worden ist. Vgl. dazu J. Śliwa, *Zur Geschichte* ..., Anm. 12 und dort zit. Lit. S. auch zuletzt A. Niwiński, *Cercueil de pretre égyptien à l'Université Jagellonne*, BIFAO 86, 1986, p. 257—266, pl. 37—38.

nicht zuletzt aus diesem Grunde nach Istanbul, da er an die Wiederherstellung der Souveränität Polens mit Hilfe der mit Rußland kämpfenden französischen, englischen, sardinischen und türkischen Armeen glaubte. Am 13. September 1855 verließ er per Schiff Marseille und gelangte über Malta und Smyrna/Izmir an den Bosporus, wo er am 22. September ankam. Adam Mickiewicz wohnte in einem Haus in Pera [12], das zum geistigen Zentrum der in der Türkei lebenden Polen sowie der diplomatischen Kreise wurde, indes nur kurze Zeit. Bereits am 26. November 1855 verstarb der Dichter in Istanbul, wahrscheinlich an der dort herrschenden Choleraepidemie.

Am Bosporus hatten sich auch zahlreiche polnische Künstler und Kaufleute niedergelassen. Zu den ersteren gehörte u. a. Stanisław Chlebowski (1835—1884), der in den Jahren 1864—1876 Hofmaler des Sultans Abdülaziz war [13]. Er schuf viele historische Schlachtenbilder, die die Geschichte der Türkei glorifizierten (u. a. *Sieg bei Warna, Einzug Mehmed II. in Konstantinopel 1453*). Zugleich malte Stanislaw Chlebowski auch orientalische Genrebilder, Landschaften und Porträts.

Von den am Bosporus lebenden polnischen Kaufleuten ist Henryk Groppler zu nennen — ein Vertreter schweizerischer Juwelier- und Uhrenfirmen und zugleich Mitbesitzer der Marmorsteinbrücke in Bandirma (am Marmara-Meer auf der asiatischen Seite) und der Boracitgrube in Alçi Maden (in Anatolien, am Wege von Bursa nach Balikesir) [14]. Seit 1847 wohnte er in seinem Hause in Bebek, einer Ortschaft auf der europäischen Seite des Bosporus, in der Nähe der Festung Rumeli Hisari, die von Mehmed II. vor dem Angriff auf Konstantinopel errichtet worden war. Sein Haus wurde zu einem Ort der Begegnungen für Polen, die die Türkei bereisten. Henryk Groppler war der Sohn des Krakauer Juweliers Krzysztof Groppler, der Marianna Zuzanna, geb. Rossberg geheiratet hatte. Deren Schwester Marianna — Joanna Karolina hatte 1826 Franciszek Ksawery Matejko geheiratet, und aus dieser Ehe entstammte der 1838 geborene Jan Matejko. Henryk Groppler war in Kraków Gast seines Vetters gewesen und hatte 1872 ihn und seine Frau Teodora nach Istanbul eingeladen.

Der damals 34-jährige Künstler, der seine ersten großen Erfolge im In- und Ausland hatte [15], nahm die Einladung bereitwillig an. Zweifellos

---

[12] Dieses Haus steht bis heute, darin befindet sich jetzt das Mickiewicz-Museum. Die Straße hieß ursprünglich Yeni Sehir. Das Haus ist 1870 abgebrannt, doch auf Anregung Henryk Gropplers, der das Grundstück gekauft hatte, wurde es wiederaufgebaut. Die Straße wurde zweideutig in Adam sokak („Straße Adams" oder auch „Straße des Menschen") benannt. Heute heißt sie Tatli Badem Sokak. 1933 wurde in das Haus eine Tafel mit einer Inschrift in polnisch und türkisch eingemauert.

[13] Vgl. J. Śliwa, *Zur Geschichte* ..., Anm. 30 und dort zit. Lit.

[14] Vgl. H. Łuczak-Kozerska, in: *PSB* 8, 1959, S. 637—638.

[15] 1865 wurde in einer Ausstellung in Paris das Bild Matejkos *Predigt Skargas* mit der goldenen Medaille und 1867 in der Weltausstellung in Paris das Bild *Rejtan* mit

lag die Ursache für die Entscheidung zum Bosporus reisen zu wollen, nicht nur in allgemeinen Streben, fremde Länder kennen zu lernen, sondern auch in zwei Faktoren begründet: Zunächst war es Möglichkeit, sich sorgenfrei bei anderen Freunden und Verwandten zu erholen, die sich der stets zur Arbeit gezwungene Künstler selbst nicht leisten konnte. Der zweite Grund war ein mehr künstlerischer. Matejko, der die Geschichte Polens darzustellen beabsichtigte, wollte den Besuch in einem Land nicht versäumen, welches nie die Teilung Polens anerkannt und über 4 Jahrhunderte hinweg anhaltenden Einfluß auf die Kultur und Kunst ausgeübt hatte. Matejko glaubte, daß das Kennenlernen der in Istanbul befindlichen Kunstwerke verschiedener Epochen für seine weitere künstlerische Entwicklung vorteilhaft sein könnte.

Am 2. September reisten Matejko mit seiner Frau zunächst von Kraków nach Wien und von dort mit einem Donaudampfschiff zwei Tage lang nach Ruščuk (z. Z. Ruse). Mit der Eisenbahn erreichten sie Warna, wo sie etwas länger verweilten, da Matejko das Schlachtfeld von 1444 sehen wollte [16]. Von Warna aus fuhr das Ehepaar dann per Schiff nach Istanbul.

Die Sehenswürdigkeiten aus verschiedenen Epochen bergende Hauptstadt der Türkei faszinierte den Künstler. Jeden Tag fuhr ein kleines Dampfschiff Gropplers, das den anspruchsvollen Namen „Herrscher" trug, vom Landungsplatz in Bebek ab, um nach drei Viertelstunden die berühmte Neue Brücke (Yeni Köprü, Pont Neuf) zu erreichen. Diese Brücke über dem Goldenen Horn verband das alte Istanbul mit den Stadtvierteln Galata und Pera. Matejko ging stundenlang durch die Stadt spazieren und hielt in seinem Skizzenbuch Fragmente der Mauer aus der Theodosius-Zeit, Kapitelle der Hagia Sophia, architektonische Details der wichtigsten Moschee — Beyazit, Süleymaniye, Sultan Valide, Nuri Osmaniye. Er fertigte Skizzen von den Stadtbewohnern, vor allem aber reizte es ihn, die Nationalitätenvielfalt der Landesbewohner festzuhalten — Türken, Griechen, Syrier, Armenier und Neger, gezeichnet zu Pferde, zu Fuss und in ihren Trachten. In einem Brief vom 27. September (Freitag) an seine Familie in der Heimat schildert Jan Matejko seine Eindrücke von der Stadt so: „Pflaster unheimlich unbequem, steile Straßen und Treppenstraßen — bei regem Straßenbetrieb und -lärm gleicht die Stadt der Vorhölle, insbesondere dann, wenn die Rauchwolken der den Bosporus befahrenden Dampfschiffe über die Galata- und Perahäuser hinwegziehen, über die sich beherrschend ein Galataturm erhebt.

---

einer Medaille ausgezeichnet. Dieses Bild wurde vom Kaiser Franz Joseph erworben. 1870 wurde Matejko die *Ehrenlegion* für das Bild *Lubliner Union* verliehen. In den nachfolgenden Jahren erhielten seine Bilder mehrmals hohe Preise in verschiedenen ausländischen Ausstellungen. 1873 wurde der Künstler Mitglied des Institut de France und der Berliner Akademie der Künste, 1878 der Rafaels Akademie in Urbino.

[16] Acht Jahre nach seinem Aufenthalt in Warna hat Matejko das Bild *Schlacht bei Warna* gemalt, das in der Nationalgalerie in Budapest aufbewahrt wird.

1. Amphoriskos. Inv.-Nr. 10.143. Photographie des Museums der Jagiellonen-Universität

2. Flakon. Inv.-Nr. 10.144. Photographie des Museums der Jagiellonen-
Universität

3. Flakon. Inv.-Nr. 10.314. Photographie des Museums der Jagiellonen-
Universität

4. Öllampe. Inv.-Nr. 10.395. Photographie
K. K. Pollesch

5. Öllampe. Inv.-Nr. 10.406. Photographie
K. K. Pollesch

6. — 7. J. Matejko, *Bleistiftskizze der Sehenswürdigkeiten Istanbuls*. Kraków, Jan-Matejko-
Haus. Nach: J. M. Michałowski, *Jan Matejko*, Warszawa 1979

8. J. Matejko, *Bebek von der Bosporusseite*. Lwów Gemäldegalerie. Nach: J. M. Michałowski, *Jan Matejko*, War-szawa 1979, Taf. 13

9. J. Matejko, *Die im Bosporus ertränkte*. Wrocław, Nationalmuseum. Nach: J. M. Michałowski, *Jan Matejko*, Warszawa 1979, Taf. 20

Die Sonne ähnelt vor ihrem Untergang einer blutigen Hostie, der dichte Passantenstrom aus Vertretern aller Nationalitäten gleicht — gerade auf der überfüllten Brücke — einer Völkerwanderung, einer Verflechtung der asiatischen mit den europäischen Sippen … Ich habe in meinem Leben Verschiedenes erlebt, aber noch nie einen so eigenartig unfaßbaren inneren Zustand wie heute. Etwas Wirklichkeitsfremdes und eine unaussprechliche Schlaftrunkenheit, eine ganze Skala von Gefühlen und Erinnerungen durchlaufen mich, ohne eine Spur zu hinterlassen … Alles wird hier mit einer Trauer oder aber mit gedankenloser, krankhafter Freude erfüllt. Friedhöfe in der Nähe von Harems und Wohnungen können meine Worte nur bestätigen … Am Dienstag (also am 1. Oktober — Anm. J. O.) mache ich einen Ausflug nach Brussa" [17]. Diese Grundstimmung Matejkos bewirkte beim Künstler eine, ihm sonst fremde Inaktivität; er malte nur ganz wenig. Während seines einmonatigen Aufenthalts entstanden, abgesehen von Bleistiftskizzen und Landschaftsnotizen (Abb. 6—7), nur zwei kleine Porträts von Herrn und Frau Groppler sowie zwei kleinformatige Bilder. Ungeachtet dessen nehmen diese Zeichnungen und die beiden Bilder einen wichtigen Platz im künstlerischen Gesamtwerk Matejkos ein. Der Künstler, der außer zeitgenössischen Porträts, nach der Erfüllung seiner patriotischen Botschaft strebend, nur mit der Geschichte Polens verbundener Bilder [18] schuf, und dies im Glauben patriotischer Pflichterfüllung, hatte während des Aufenthalts in der Türkei seine einzige Landschaft nach der Natur *Bebek von der Bosporusseite* (Abb. 8) und den einzigen weiblichen Akt *Die im Bosporus Ertränkte*, genannt auch *Hassan ertränkt seine untreue Frau* (Abb. 9) gemalt [19]. Diese beiden Bilder bezeugen Matejkos grosses Talent, seine Veranlagung zur Vielseitigkeit. Indes dominierend war beim Künstler seine Orientierung auf historisierende Gemälde. Seine im Atelier gemalten historischen Schlachtenbilder waren in einer Weise gemalt, die es ihm ermöglichte, Ausdruckskraft und im

---

[17] Zitiert nach S. Serafinska, *Matejko. Wspomnienia rodzinne.* Kraków 1955, S. 394—396.

[18] Zum Matejkos Lebenslauf vgl. A. Bochnak, *Matejko*, in: *PSB* 20, 1975, S. 184—191. Eine durch die Geschichte anderer Völker angeregte Thematik vertreten lediglich 4 Bilder: *Iwan der Schreckliche, Jan Wilczek* (tschechischer Held — Anm. J. O.) *während der Verteidigung des Klosters vor den Ungarn, Johanna d'Arc* und *Der hl. Ludwig in den Kreuzzug ziehend.*

[19] Dieses Bild hat ein merkwürdiges Schicksal erlebt. Die erste in Istanbul gemalte Version hat Matejko Chlebowski geschenkt, der von diesem Bild begeistert war. Dieser gab (oder verkaufte) es dem französischen Maler J. L. Gérome, welcher es wiederum seinem Schwiegervater Adolf Goupil, dem bekannten Pariser Antiquitätenhändler übergab. Das weitere Schicksal ist unbekannt. 1880 hat Matejko eine zweite Version dieses Bildes (88 × 134 cm) gemalt, wo die Gesichtszüge des Türken denen des Künstlers und die ertränkte Odaliske seiner Frau Teodora ähneln. Bis 1945 befand sich dieses Bild in der Gemäldegalerie in Lwów (wo bis heute *Bebek* aufbewahrt wird), heute — im Nationalmuseum in Wrocław.

Geneseprozeß seiner Bilder Kompositionsdekorativität überzeugend zu vereinen und vor Augen zu führen. Deswegen hat der Künstler auf die natürliche Perspektive, das natürliche Spiel der Lichter, der Schatten und der Farben, auf all das, was auf den beiden kleinen am Bosporus gemalten Bildern zum Ausdruck kommt, verzichtet. Die Wirklichkeit ist dort so gezeigt, wie sie der von ihrer Schönheit bezauberte Künstler sah. Sie wurde von der Phantasie des Schöpfers der historischen Dramen nicht umgearbeitet. *Bebek* enthält einige Elemente, mit denen sich dieses Landschaftsbild an die sich damals entwickelnde impressionistische Malerei nähert. Auch aus diesem Grunde wirft die kurze türkische Episode im Leben Matejkos, der seine Zeit zwischen Kraków, Paris, Wien und Berlin teilte, ein neues Licht auf die schöpferischen Möglichkeiten und Fähigkeiten des Künstlers.

Matejko hat von seiner Reise nur wenige Andenken mitgebracht — Orientteppiche und Gewebefragmente, kleine Souvenirs und Photographien osmanischer architektonischer Denkmäler [20]. Zu den bleibenden Andenken gehört die Photographie der beiden Ehepaare (Groppler und Matejko), die bei „Abdullah frères à Péra, photographe de Sa Majesté le Sultan" gemacht worden ist (Abb. 10). Unter den aus der Türkei mitgebrachten Gegenständen befinden sich auch drei kleine römische Gefäße, und zwei römische Lampen die typisch für kleinasiatische Werkstätte sind, die vielleicht in Brussa gekauft worden sind [21]. Die Antike vermochte Matejko nicht zu faszinieren, er malte keine antiken Motive und beabsichtigte auch nicht, historische Gemälde der antiken Geschichte zu schaffen. In seinen Briefen aus Italien 1878 finden sich keine bewundernden Worte für antike Architektur oder antike Skulptur. Auch in seinen Skizzenbüchern gibt es keine Zeichnung von griechischen oder römischen Denkmälern. Aus welchem Grunde hat er diese Objekte gekauft (bekommen oder gefunden) und nach Kraków mitgebracht? Es scheint, daß nur eine Antwort darauf gegeben werden kann: Damals war gerade das Archäologische Kabinett der Jagiellonen-Universität eingerichtet worden, mit dessen Direktor, Prof. J. Łepkowski, er befreundet war. Matejko wußte, daß der Denkmäler-bestand des Kabinetts noch klein war und jede Gabe (und der Künstler

---

[20] Diese Gegenstände und Photographien befinden sich im Krakauer Haus Jan Matejkos. Der Verfasser möchte an dieser Stelle Frau Maria Przemecka-Zielińska, Kustos des Matejko-Hauses für die zur Verfügung gestellten Materialien aussprechen herzlich danken. Die Photographien der osmanischen Architektur beweisen, daß Matejko beabsichtigte, ein Bild aus der polnisch-türkischen Geschichte zu malen, vielleicht die Endepisode aus dem Leben des in Istanbul im 17. Jh. verhafteten und hingerichteten Dymitr Wiśniowiecki.

[21] Die genaue Herkunft ist nicht bekannt. Es steht auch nicht fest, ob der Amphoriskos (zitiert in der Anm. 2, Punkt 1), tatsächlich aus Ephesus stammt, wo Matejko nie gewesen ist. Vielleicht hat der dieses Objekt Verkaufende dem Antiquitätenhändler eine solche Angabe gemacht!

hatte für den Unterhalt einer großen Familie zu sorgen und daher sein Leben lang Geldprobleme) mit Freude angenommen wurde, die zur Erweiterung der Lehrsammlung über die antike Keramik beitrug. Er war der Meinung, daß die Bereicherung der Sammlungen der ältesten polnischen Universität die Pflicht eines jeden Polen sei. So dachten auch viele in und außerhalb Galizien lebende Landsleute.

Im gleichen Jahr, in dem Matejko in die Türkei reiste, beendete er auch seinen berühmten *Kopernikus*, ein Bild, das aus den öffentlichen Sammlungen für die Universität erworben wurde. Mehr als ein Jahrzehnt später (1887) verlieh die Jagiellonen-Universität Jan Matejko in Anerkennung seiner Verdienste die Würde eines Ehrendoktors. Die aus der Türkei mitgebrachte bescheidene Gabe war sein persönlicher Beitrag zur Entfaltung der polnischen klassischen Archäologie.